MORTAR
& PESTLE

MORTAR
& PESTLE

65 DELICIOUS RECIPES FOR SAUCES, RUBS, MARINADES, AND MORE

RYLAND PETERS & SMALL
LONDON • NEW YORK

Art director Leslie Harrington
Senior editor Gillian Haslam
Head of production Patricia Harrington
Editorial director Julia Charles
Publisher Cindy Richards
Indexer Hilary Bird

First published in 2021 by
Ryland Peters & Small
20–21 Jockey's Fields, London WC1R 4BW
and
341 E 116th St, New York NY 10029
www.rylandpeters.com

10 9 8 7 6 5 4 3 2

Recipe collection compiled by Julia Charles

Text copyright © Valerie Aikman-Smith, Ghillie
Basan, Fiona Beckett, Jordan Bourke, Chloe
Coker & Jane Montgomery, Philip Dennhardt
& Kristin Jensen, Ursula Ferrigno, Amy Ruth
Finegold, Mat Follas, Liz Franklin, Felipe
Fuentes Cruz & Ben Fordham, Nicola Graimes,
Dunja Gulin, Carol Hilker, Kathy Kordalis,
Jenny Linford, Nitisha Patel, Louise Pickford,
James Porter, Laura Santtini, Janet Sawyer,
Laura Washburn-Hutton 2021

Design and photographs copyright © Ryland
Peters & Small 2021

ISBN: 978-1-78879-349-0

Printed in China

A CIP record for this book is available
from the British Library.
US Library of Congress Cataloging-in-
Publication Data has been applied for.

Notes:
• Both British (Metric) and American (Imperial
plus US cups) are included in these recipes for
your convenience, however it is important to
work with one set of measurements and not
alternate between the two within a recipe.
• All spoon measurements are level unless
otherwise specified.
• All eggs are medium (UK) or large (US).
Uncooked or partially cooked eggs should not
be served to the very old, frail, young children,
pregnant women or those with compromised
immune systems.
• Ovens should be preheated to the specified
temperatures. We recommend using an oven
thermometer. If using a fan-assisted oven,
adjust temperatures according to the
manufacturer's instructions.
• When a recipe calls for the grated zest of
citrus fruit, buy unwaxed fruit and wash well
before using. If you can only find treated fruit,
scrub well in warm soapy water before using.
• To sterilize preserving jars, wash them in hot,
soapy water and rinse in boiling water. Place
in a large saucepan and cover with hot water.
With the saucepan lid on, bring the water to
a boil and continue boiling for 15 minutes. Turn
off the heat and leave the jars in the hot water
until just before they are to be filled. Invert
the jars onto a clean dish towel to dry.
Sterilize the lids for 5 minutes, by boiling or
according to the manufacturer's instructions.
Jars should be filled and sealed while they are
still hot.

MIX
Paper | Supporting
responsible forestry
FSC® C008047

CONTENTS

INTRODUCTION

Incredible flavors, inspiring ingredients, simple techniques—learn how to master the mortar and pestle and bring new sophistication to your cooking with 65 delicious recipes. The mortar and pestle are ancient tools that no modern kitchen should be without—they're handy for everything from cracking peppercorns and bruising fresh herbs to making sauces, marinades, spice pastes, and dry rubs. This book brings you an array of enticing recipes from around the world, all of which employ a mortar and pestle to bring creative seasoning and exciting new techniques to your home cooking.

The book begins with a chapter on sauces and condiments, with recipes for pestos, oils, mustards, relishes, and salsas—keep a stock of these in your fridge or pantry and you can add instant flavor and interest to the simplest of meals. A section on snacks and small bites follows, with hard-to-resist savory treats. The poultry and game chapter features an array of Asian curries with an intensity of heat ranging from hot and fiery to warming and spicy, plus new ways to cook chicken wings and tagine dishes flavored with North African harissa. In the meat chapter, you'll find ideas to enliven weekend roasts, such as stuffed porchetta or spiced leg of lamb cooked in a salt crust, plus quick weekday meals. The fish and seafood chapter has an exciting selection of tempting recipes, from hot and sour fish soup to salt-cured gravadlax, fish tacos, and indulgent grilled lobsters. If you are looking for new ideas for side dishes and vegetarian meals, try the butternut squash tagine, miso borscht with gremolata, honey and ras el hanout roots, or shaved broccoli and buckwheat salad with dukkah.

Once you have learned how to make your own seasonings, sauces, rubs, and pastes using a mortar and pestle, you'll never want to buy readymade again.

SAUCES
& CONDIMENTS

PESTOS

Pestos make fantastic sauces for freshly cooked pasta, but can also add color and flavor to a wide variety of other dishes. Use them as you would a relish to spice up simple fritattas and quiches, serve them spread on crostini as attractive canapés, or spread them on fresh bread for a quick and tasty snack.

TRADITIONAL PESTO

¾ cup/100 g pine nuts
¾ cup/50 g finely grated Parmesan cheese
2 oz./50 g sheep's milk cheese (or strong Cheddar cheese)
2 garlic cloves
leaves from a large bunch of fresh basil
olive oil, to drizzle
sea salt, to taste

DILL & LEMON PESTO

¾ cup/100 g walnuts
3½ oz./100 g soft goats' cheese
1 garlic clove
a large bunch of fresh dill
first-press rapeseed oil, to drizzle
grated zest and freshly squeezed juice of 1 lemon
sea salt, to taste

WILD GARLIC PESTO

¾ cup/100 g hazelnuts
¾ cup/50 g finely grated Parmesan cheese
2 oz./50 g strong Cheddar cheese
3½ oz./100 g ramps/wild garlic flowers
first-press rapeseed oil, to drizzle
grated zest of 1 lemon
freshly squeezed juice of ½ lemon
sea salt, to taste

KALE PESTO

¾ cup/100 g cashew nuts
1¼ cups/100 g finely grated Parmesan cheese
2 garlic cloves
a large bunch of fresh kale, stalks removed
olive oil, to drizzle
sea salt, to taste

EACH RECIPE MAKES 4–6 SERVINGS

For each pesto, put the nuts, a pinch of sea salt, the cheese, and garlic (but not the ramps/wild garlic flowers) in a mortar and pestle and pound to a smooth paste. Add the leaves and any zest and grind again. Add any lemon juice and oil as required to blend until a pesto is formed—it should have the consistency to hold together when it is pressed between spoons.

Although pestos are best served when freshly made, they will keep for up to 3 days, stored in an airtight container (preferably a screwtop jar) in the fridge. More pesto recipes overleaf.

ROASTED BEET PESTO

1 large roasted beet/beetroot
1 tablespoon chopped fresh dill
grated zest of ½ a lemon
freshly squeezed juice of 1 lemon
a handful of fresh flat-leaf parsley leaves
a handful of arugula/rocket
1 garlic clove
2 tablespoons extra virgin olive oil
¾ cup/100 g toasted walnuts
2 teaspoons capers
1 tablespoon cream cheese (optional)

RICOTTA & HERB PESTO

9 oz./250 g ricotta (see page 141 if you wish
    to make your own)
a large handful of fresh flat-leaf parsley leaves
a large handful of fresh mint leaves
grated zest of 1 lemon
freshly squeezed juice of 2 lemons
2 garlic cloves
2 fresh red chiles/chillies
salt and freshly ground black pepper
toasted pine nuts, for sprinkling

WATERCRESS PESTO

a large handful of watercress (about 1 cup/50 g)
grated zest of 1 lemon,
freshly squeezed lemon juice, to taste
⅓ cup/50 g blanched almonds, toasted
6 tablespoons extra virgin olive oil
about ⅓ cup/20 g grated Parmesan cheese
1 garlic clove
salt and freshly ground black pepper

EACH RECIPE MAKES 4–6 SERVINGS

MUSHROOM & WALNUT PESTO

4½–5½ cups/320 g chestnut mushrooms, fried
    in 1 tablespoon olive oil
2 garlic cloves
2 tablespoons walnut oil
½ teaspoon dried rosemary
1 fresh red chile/chilli
freshly squeezed juice of ½ a lemon
a handful of fresh flat-leaf parsley leaves
¾ cup/100 g walnuts

For each pesto, finely chop all of the ingredients and pound them together in a large mortar and pestle until a pesto is formed—it should have the consistency to hold together when it is pressed between spoons.

Although pestos are best served when freshly made, they will keep for up to 3 days, stored in an airtight container (preferably a screwtop jar) in the fridge.

GREMOLATA

Gremolata is an Italian condiment that works with literally every pizza and you can use the leftovers to sprinkle on top of pasta or soups. It looks best when everything is chopped very finely and uniformly. Having said that, though, you can leave the parsley a bit bigger than the garlic for a more rustic look.

a large bunch of fresh flat-leaf
    parsley
1 garlic clove
zest of 1 lemon

MAKES ¾ CUP/30 G

Strip the parsley leaves off the stalks. Make sure the leaves are completely dry before chopping them as finely as you can. Transfer to the mortar.

Chop the garlic as finely as you can, otherwise you might bite on a big bit of raw garlic, which isn't very nice. Add to the mortar with the lemon zest, then blend everything together with the pestle until well combined. Store any leftovers in an airtight container in the fridge for a day or two.

POUNDED PARSLEY & GARLIC OIL

When using a mortar and pestle, don't be afraid to make a lot of noise! The more you pound the parsley, garlic, and chile/chilli, the better the oil will taste because you're releasing more of the volatile aromatics than if you just chop them.

4–6 heaped tablespoons chopped
    fresh flat-leaf parsley
1 small garlic clove
½ teaspoon finely diced fresh chile/
    chilli or hot red pepper/chilli
    flakes (optional)
pinch of fine sea salt
½–¾ cup/120–180 ml good-quality
    olive oil

MAKES ½–¾ CUP/125–180 ML

Put the parsley, garlic, chile/chilli (if using), and salt in a mortar and pestle. Pound together really, really well, until it forms a paste, then pound some more for good measure before mixing in ½ cup/120 ml of the olive oil.

Check the consistency and decide if you want to add some or all of the remaining oil. Pour the oil into a sterilized jar (see page 4). Seal the jar and store the oil in the fridge for up to 1 month. It might turn cloudy from the cold, but bring it back to room temperature before you want to use it and it will turn clear again.

PROVENÇAL OLIVE RELISH

This tapenade is Provence in a jar! The olives are drenched in oil and spiced with capers and salty anchovies. It works perfectly on bruschetta, pizzas, crudités, and pickled eggs, or lightly spread on chicken before roasting in the oven..

2 cups/200 g pitted/stoned Kalamata
    olives, drained
12 anchovy fillets
¼ cup/40 g capers, drained
grated zest and freshly squeezed
    juice of 1 lemon
¼ cup/60 ml extra virgin olive oil,
    plus extra to cover
cracked black pepper

MAKES 3 CUPS (24 OZ.)/700 ML

Place all the ingredients in a mortar and pestle and blend until the mixture is almost smooth but still has some texture. Season with pepper.

Pack the tapenade into sterilized glass jars (see page 4) and drizzle with a little olive oil to cover the surface. Seal with an airtight lid and store in the fridge for up to 6 months.

LEMON & DILL MUSTARD

Lemon and dill lend a delicate flavor to all things, especially mustard. Add a spoonful to pan-fried salmon to make a zingy accompanying sauce, or stir a spoonful into mayonnaise or crème fraîche to serve with burgers.

1 cup/150 g yellow mustard seeds
1 cup/235 ml lemon verbena vinegar
¼ cup/85 g clear honey
grated zest and freshly squeezed
   juice of 1 lemon
¼ cup/10 g fresh dill, roughly
   chopped
a pinch of sea salt

MAKES 2 CUPS (16 OZ.)/475 ML

Dry-roast the mustard seeds in a hot skillet/frying pan over a high heat for 2 minutes. Place the roasted seeds and vinegar in a ceramic bowl and set aside to soak for 12–14 hours or overnight.

Put the soaked mustard seeds, honey, zest, lemon juice, and dill in a mortar and pestle and blend until smooth. Add a little more vinegar if the mix is a little thick. Season with salt.

Pour into sterilized glass jars (see page 4) and screw the lids on tightly. Store in the fridge for up to 2 months.

MÉDOC MUSTARD

Médoc is a red wine from the Bordeaux region of France, and is a good, robust wine to use in mustards. You can really use any good red wine. Don't be tempted to use a cheap one—it won't work.

½ cup/75 g yellow mustard seeds
½ cup/75 g brown mustard seeds
¾ cup/180 ml Médoc or other red
   wine
¼ cup/60 ml red wine vinegar
¼ cup/85 g clear honey
2 garlic cloves, roughly chopped
a pinch of sea salt

MAKES 2 CUPS (16 OZ.)/475 ML

Dry-roast the mustard seeds in a hot skillet/frying pan over a high heat for 2 minutes. Place the roasted seeds and vinegar in a ceramic bowl and soak overnight.

Put the soaked mustard seeds, wine, vinegar, honey, and garlic in a mortar and pestle and blend until smooth. Add a little more vinegar if the mix is a little thick. Season with salt.

Pour into sterilized glass jars (see page 4) and screw the lids on tightly. Store in the fridge for up to 2 months.

ROSEMARY & THYME MUSTARD

Rosemary and thyme bring a wonderful Mediterranean herbal flavor to mustard. Try spreading this mustard over a whole chicken before roasting to add flavor to the skin.

1 cup/150 g yellow mustard seeds
1 cup/235 ml apple cider vinegar
¼ cup/85 g clear honey
1 tablespoon fresh rosemary leaves, chopped
2 tablespoons fresh thyme leaves
a pinch of sea salt

MAKES 2 CUPS (16 OZ.)/475 ML

Dry-roast the mustard seeds in a hot skillet/frying pan over a high heat for 2 minutes. Place the roasted seeds and vinegar in a ceramic bowl and soak overnight.

Put the soaked mustard seeds, honey, and rosemary and thyme leaves in a mortar and pestle and blend until smooth. Add a little more vinegar if the mix is a little thick. Season with salt.

Pour into sterilized glass jars (see page 4) and screw the lids on tightly. Store in the fridge for up to 2 months.

WHOLEGRAIN MUSTARD

Good wholegrain mustards can be hard to find and also a little expensive. This is really good basic recipe that you can add wines, spices, and herbs to. It's particularly good on a steak sandwich.

½ cup/75 g yellow mustard seeds
½ cup/75 g brown mustard seeds
1 cup/235 ml red wine vinegar
¼ cup/85 g clear honey
1 garlic clove, finely chopped
a pinch of sea salt

MAKES 2 CUPS (16 OZ.)/475 ML

Dry-roast the mustard seeds in a hot skillet/frying pan over a high heat for 2 minutes. Place the roasted seeds and vinegar in a ceramic bowl and soak overnight.

Put the soaked mustard seeds, honey, and garlic in a mortar and pestle and pound until you have a grainy mustard. Add a little more vinegar if the mix is a little thick. Season with salt.

Pour into sterilized glass jars (see page 4) and screw the lids on tightly. Store in the fridge for up to 2 months.

ROASTED TOMATILLO SALSA

No self-respecting Mexican restaurant, or household, is without a good salsa. It goes with everything so make a big batch and never let it run out!

1–2 fresh green chiles/chillies (such as serrano or Thai green), stalks removed
2 garlic cloves, peeled
2–3 fresh tomatillos, husks removed (or canned tomatillos)
1 teaspoon rock salt
3 tablespoons freshly chopped cilantro/coriander
½ onion, chopped

MAKES 6–8 SERVINGS

Preheat the oven to 400°F (200°C) Gas 6.

Put the chiles/chillies, garlic, and fresh tomatillos on a baking sheet and roast for 20 minutes or until charred. If using canned tomatillos, don't roast them, but add them at the grinding stage instead.

Halve the chiles/chillies and scoop out and discard the seeds. Using a mortar and pestle, pound the chiles/chillies, garlic, and salt into a paste. Add the tomatillos and grind until well mixed. Add the cilantro/coriander and onion and stir. Add a little water or extra salt, if required.

SALSA VERDE

Salsa verde is a versatile sauce that tastes good with absolutely everything.

3 anchovy fillets in oil, drained
1 garlic clove, peeled
2 tablespoons capers, drained
zest of 1 lemon
3 tablespoons finely chopped fresh flat-leaf parsley leaves
1 tablespoon finely chopped fresh mint leaves
1 tablespoon finely chopped arugula/rocket
½ teaspoon fine sea salt
½ cup/120 ml extra virgin olive oil
1 teaspoon Dijon mustard

MAKES ¾ CUP/180 ML

Put the anchovies, garlic, and capers in a mortar and pestle and pound into a fine paste. Transfer to a glass or ceramic bowl with the lemon zest, herbs, arugula/rocket, and salt and stir to combine, then mix in the olive oil and mustard at the end. Stir well so that all the ingredients come together nicely.

Let the salsa verde sit for about 10 minutes to allow the flavors to marry together, then taste and adjust the seasoning. Store any leftovers in a clean jar in the fridge for up to a week.

RED SALSA

Almost a cross between Hawaiian chile/chilli pepper water and a Mexican hot sauce such as Cholula, this is the best thing to go along with anything from quesadillas and fish tacos to swirling over a ceviche or serving with burgers.

6 long red chiles/chillies
3 garlic cloves, peeled
1 tablespoon cumin seeds
14-oz./400-g can whole Italian tomatoes
salt

4 x 5-oz./150-ml bottles

MAKES 6 SERVINGS

Heat up a cast-iron pan until fairly hot. Dry toast the chiles/chillies in the pan until lightly charred on all sides. Toast the garlic in the pan at the same time. Set aside.

Dry toast the cumin seeds in a small pan until they take on a little color, but watch they don't burn. Grind the seeds using a mortar and pestle.

Add the chiles/chillies, garlic, and tomatoes to the mortar and pound until you have a smooth purée. Add salt to taste. Allow to cool and stir in some water to loosen the salsa to an easy drizzling consistency.

Pour the warm sauce into sterilized bottles (see page 4) and close the seals or lids. Store in a dry place, out of the light. Once open, keep the bottle in the fridge and use within 1 week. If not storing in bottles, store in the fridge and use within 1 week.

BALACHUNG MYANMAR

A must-have condiment in Burmese cooking, this salty, spicy, crispy dish is served with almost every meal. It is delicious strewn over any noodle dish or served with rice.

50 g/¼ cup dried shrimp
6 tablespoons peanut (or vegetable) oil
2 Asian shallots, thinly sliced
2 garlic cloves, sliced
2-inch/5-cm piece of fresh ginger, peeled and thinly sliced
2–3 teaspoons hot red pepper/chilli flakes
1 tablespoon shrimp paste

MAKES ABOUT ¼ CUP/55 G

Grind the dried shrimp to a paste using a mortar and pestle and set aside.

Heat the oil in a wok set over a medium–high heat and fry the shallots for 4–5 minutes, until crisp and golden. Remove the shallots from the oil using a slotted spoon and drain on paper towels, leaving the pan over the heat.

Add the garlic, ginger, and hot red pepper/chilli flakes to the hot oil and cook for 2–3 minutes, until crisp and golden. Remove with a slotted spoon and drain on paper towels, again leaving the pan over the heat.

Stir in the ground dried shrimp and the shrimp paste and stir-fry for 2–3 minutes, until fragrant. Return the shallots and garlic mixture to the pan and stir gently until you a have a slightly sticky mixture. Cool completely before scattering over your favorite noodle dish.

The balachung can be stored in an airtight container in the fridge for up to 2 weeks.

NUOC CHAM

A classic Vietnamese sauce served with everything from salads and soups to stir-fries. There are countless variations of this sauce but all are hot, salty, sweet, and sour—flavors so beloved in South-east Asia.

2 large red chiles/chillies, chopped
2 red bird's eye chiles/chillies, deseeded and chopped
2 garlic cloves
4 tablespoons grated palm sugar
4 tablespoons Thai fish sauce
grated zest and freshly squeezed juice of 4 limes
salt and pepper

MAKES ABOUT ½ CUP/100 ML

Put the chiles/chillies, garlic, and palm sugar in a mortar and pestle and pound or blend to form a paste. Transfer to a mixing bowl and whisk in the remaining ingredients.

Store in an airtight container in the fridge and use as required.

GREEN NAM JIM

The Thai equivalent to nuoc cham, this sauce is made with green chiles/chillies for a striking contrast to the Vietnamese alternative, but red or green can be used, as desired.

2 green bird's eye chiles/chillies, deseeded and roughly chopped
4 garlic cloves, chopped
a large pinch of salt
2 tablespoons chopped fresh cilantro/coriander
4 tablespoons grated palm sugar
4 tablespoons Thai fish sauce
4 tablespoons freshly squeezed lime juice

MAKES ABOUT ½ CUP/100 ML

Put the chiles/chillies, garlic, and salt in a mortar and pestle and pound or blend to form a paste. Transfer to a mixing bowl and stir in the cilantro/coriander, palm sugar, fish sauce, and lime juice, and stir until the sugar is dissolved.

Store in an airtight container in the fridge and use as required.

SNACKS
& SMALL BITES

FURIKAKE POPCORN

Furikake is a Japanese seasoning typically made with toasted sesame seeds, nori, salt, and sugar. Try using the best natural popcorn you can find and avoid the ones that are packaged with butter substitutes.

2 tablespoons furikake seasoning
2 tablespoons sesame seeds
1 tablespoon vegetable oil
5½ oz./150 g chicken skin, e.g. the skin from 2 leg joints
½ teaspoon Maldon sea salt
7 tablespoons/100 g salted butter
1 tablespoon coconut oil
¾ cup/150 g good-quality natural or plain popcorn kernels (definitely not the microwave-in-a-bag variety)

SERVES 2

Grind the furikake seasoning with the sesame seeds using a mortar and pestle. Set aside.

Heat the vegetable oil in a pan and add the chicken skin. Gently fry until golden and crispy, then drain and cool on paper towels. Place in the mortar and pestle and pound with the salt to a breadcrumb consistency. Set aside.

Melt the butter in a small pan. Set aside.

Heat the coconut oil in a large, heavy-based lidded pan until fairly hot. Put a few kernels of popcorn in the pan. When they pop, add the rest and spread out in the oil. Put the lid on and leave the pan undisturbed for at least 30 seconds. When you hear the corn starting to pop, start shaking the pan to avoid it burning (lift it off the heat if necessary). Before fully popped, carefully lift the lid to let steam out, to avoid moisture forming on the popcorn.

Mix the melted butter into the popcorn, add the furikake mixture and mix all with the chicken skin. Tip into a bowl and serve.

MATCHSTICK FRIES
WITH SICHUAN PEPPER SALT

Super-skinny and delicate, matchsticks are an upmarket version of fries, perfect served as a substantial bar snack with a cold glass of beer.

2 large floury potatoes, roughly the same size
cornstarch/cornflour
vegetable or sunflower oil

SICHUAN PEPPER SALT
1 tablespoon Sichuan peppercorns
2 tablespoons coarse rock salt

SERVES 4 AS A SNACK

For the Sichuan Pepper Salt, heat the peppercorns in a small skillet/frying pan until hot but not smoking. Transfer to a plate to cool. Combine with the salt and grind using a mortar and pestle. Set aside.

Peel the potatoes and trim on all sides to get a block. Cut the block into thin slices, then cut the slices thinly into matchsticks.

Put the potatoes into a bowl of iced water for at least 5 minutes, to remove excess starch and prevent sticking when frying. Put the cornstarch/cornflour in a shallow bowl.

Fill a large saucepan one-third full with the oil or, if using a deep-fat fryer, follow the manufacturer's instructions. Heat the oil to 375°F (190°C) or until a cube of bread browns in 30 seconds.

Drain the potatoes and dry very well, then toss to coat lightly with the cornstarch/cornflour. Put in a strainer/sieve to help shake off any excess cornstarch/cornflour.

Working in batches, fry about a handful of potatoes at a time. Place the potatoes in a frying basket, lower into the hot oil carefully, and fry for about 5 minutes. Remove and drain on paper towels. Repeat until all of the potatoes have been fried.

Sprinkle with the Sichuan Pepper Salt and serve.

SLOW-ROASTED GARLIC, CHEESE & SICHUAN PEPPERCORN TOASTS

Slow-roasting garlic is something that can easily be done when you have the oven on to cook other dishes. It gives off a lovely aroma but, even better, provides a wonderful savory ingredient for all sorts of dishes. The garlic cooks in its own juices and can be stored in the fridge for several days. Squeeze the roast garlic paste from each clove and add it to soups, pasta sauces, and, as here, put it on toast with cheese and peppercorns.

1 garlic bulb
4 slices of sourdough bread
salted butter, to spread
½ cup/50 g shredded/grated strong
    Cheddar cheese
⅔ cup/50 g grated Parmesan cheese
1 tablespoon Sichuan peppercorns

SERVES 4

Preheat the oven to 350°F (180°C) Gas 4.

Wrap the whole bulb of garlic in kitchen foil, place on a baking sheet, and cook in the preheated oven for 45 minutes.

Preheat the broiler/grill to medium. Lightly toast and butter the sourdough slices.

Carefully squeeze 1–3 garlic cloves onto each toast; spread the garlic evenly and place the toasts on a baking sheet. Sprinkle the grated cheeses over the top of the toasts.

Crush or grind the peppercorns lightly using a mortar and pestle and sprinkle over the toasts.

Put the toasts under the preheated broiler/grill for a few minutes until the cheese is bubbling and starting to brown. Keep your eye on them as they can turn quickly. Serve immediately.

PAN-FRIED CHICKPEA FRITTERS

Simple and quick, these fritters are perfect served as a casual snack, or add a side salad for a light lunch. You can also experiment a little, by adding in or substituting your favorite herbs or spices. Corn and little chunks of chorizo are a delicious alternative to the chickpeas.

2 teaspoons cumin seeds
½ teaspoon hot red pepper/chilli flakes
1 cup/250 g soy or Greek yogurt
1 tablespoon pure maple syrup
sea salt
1 cup/120 g spelt flour (white or wholegrain)
½ teaspoon baking powder
¾ cup/170 ml rice, soy, or dairy milk
1 egg, lightly beaten
14-oz./400-g can of chickpeas, drained and rinsed
1 small red onion, finely chopped
a small handful of fresh flat-leaf parsley, finely chopped
a small handful of cilantro/coriander, finely chopped
olive or vegetable oil, for frying
1 scallion/spring onion, finely sliced diagonally
extra virgin olive oil, for drizzling

MAKES 16

In a dry skillet/frying pan, gently fry the cumin seeds over a medium heat until aromatic. Pound half of them to a powder using a mortar and pestle (keep the other half to one side). In a bowl, mix together the ground cumin, hot red pepper/chilli flakes, yogurt, maple syrup, and a good pinch of sea salt. Set to one side.

Place the flour and baking powder in a large bowl, slowly whisk in the milk and beaten egg, until well combined with no lumps. Add in the chickpeas, red onion, almost all of the herbs, the remaining cumin seeds, ¾ teaspoon sea salt, and a few grindings of black pepper. Stir everything together to combine.

Place 1 tablespoon of olive or vegetable oil in a large, non-stick skillet/frying pan and set over a medium-high heat. Once hot, add 2 level tablespoons of batter for each fritter. Fry in batches, without overcrowding the pan, for about 5 minutes, turning once, until they are golden brown and cooked through.

To serve, pile the fritters up on individual plates and scatter over the sliced scallions/spring onions and extra herbs. Finally, drizzle over some extra virgin olive oil. Spoon the yogurt mixture over the top or serve it in a bowl on the side.

POLENTA FRIES WITH PESTO

Polenta can be notoriously bland if you don't get some oomph into the mixture with well-flavored stock and lots of Parmesan. These "fries" are served with a beautifully fresh pesto to make a very more-ish snack.

500 ml/2 cups good-quality stock
¾ cup/125 g fine quick-cook polenta
2 tablespoons/30 g butter
⅔ cup/50 g finely grated Parmesan
   cheese
sunflower oil, for frying

FRESH BASIL PESTO
2 large handfuls of fresh basil leaves
2 garlic cloves
½ cup/120 ml extra virgin olive oil
zest of 1 lemon and freshly squeezed
   juice of ½
⅔ cup/50 g finely grated Parmesan
   cheese
sea salt flakes

SERVES 6

Bring the stock to a boil in a saucepan, turn the heat down, and slowly add the polenta, stirring all the time. Stir until the polenta is thick and smooth and comes away from the sides of the pan. Remove from the heat and stir in the butter and Parmesan. Spread the polenta onto a lightly oiled baking sheet to a depth of about ½ inch/1 cm. Leave to set and when completely cold, cut into rectangular "fries" using a sharp knife.

To make the pesto, pound the basil, garlic, and oil together using a mortar and pestle to make a paste. Add the lemon zest, juice, and Parmesan. Mix well and season with sea salt. Tip into a serving bowl.

Pour the sunflower oil into a deep saucepan and heat to 375°F (190°C). Fry the polenta until golden and crisp. Drain on paper towels and serve immediately, with the bowl of pesto for dipping. (If you find these fries addictive but wish to ring the changes, take a look at the pesto variations on pages 10–13.)

POULTRY & GAME

CHICKEN LAKSA

Hailing from south-east Asia, laksa is a spicy noodle soup made with coconut milk. It is always adorned with a selection of garnishes. The noodles and other specialist ingredients can be found in Asian stores and larger supermarkets.

9 oz./250 g dried rice stick noodles
2 large skinless chicken breast fillets
    (about 12 oz./350 g)
1¾ pints/1 litre chicken stock
2 tablespoons vegetable oil
1⅔ cups/400 ml canned coconut milk
¾ cup/200 ml coconut cream
2 tablespoons fish sauce
2 teaspoons granulated/caster sugar

LAKSA PASTE

2 teaspoons coriander seeds
6 shallots, chopped
4 garlic cloves, chopped
2 lemon grass stalks, thinly sliced
2 large red bird's eye chiles/chillies,
    deseeded and sliced
1-inch/2.5-cm piece of fresh
    galangal, peeled and chopped
1-inch/2.5-cm piece of fresh
    turmeric, peeled and chopped
    (or 1 teaspoon ground turmeric)
4 macadamia nuts
1 tablespoon shrimp paste

TO SERVE

beansprouts, trimmed
½ cucumber, sliced
deep-fried puffed tofu
deep-fried shallots
fresh cilantro/coriander or mint
1 lime, cut into wedges
sambal olek or chili/chilli oil

SERVES 4

Soak the dried noodles in a bowl of hot water for 20–30 minutes until softened. Drain well, shake dry, and set aside.

Put the chicken breasts in a saucepan with the stock set over a low-medium heat. Simmer very gently for 10 minutes until the chicken is just cooked.

Remove the chicken from the stock and set aside to cool completely. Once cool, slice thinly. Reserve the stock.

To make the laksa paste, toast the coriander seeds in a dry skillet/frying pan until fragrant, then grind in a mortar and pestle. Add the remaining paste ingredients and pound until smooth.

Heat the oil in a wok or non-stick saucepan set over a medium heat and add the laksa paste. Fry for 2 minutes until fragrant, then add the coconut milk and reserved chicken stock. Simmer gently for 10 minutes, then stir in the coconut cream, fish sauce, and sugar. Simmer gently for a further 2–3 minutes.

Divide the noodles between bowls and add the sliced chicken. Pour over the hot soup and serve topped with a selection of garnishes. Pass around a pot of sambal olek or chili/chilli oil, to drizzle.

MALAYSIAN CHICKEN & POTATO CURRY

This Malaysian chicken curry is a gloriously aromatic affair, given creamy richness by the coconut milk, while the new potatoes soak up the spicy gravy in the nicest possible way. Serve with jasmine or basmati rice for a delicious meal.

2 lemon grass stalks
3 tablespoons oil
2 onions, finely chopped
2 garlic cloves, chopped
¾-inch/2-cm piece of fresh ginger, peeled and finely chopped
8 chicken thighs
1¾ cups/400 ml canned coconut milk
4 kaffir lime leaves
1 cinnamon stick
8 small new potatoes
salt

CURRY POWDER
1 star anise
1 teaspoon fennel seeds
4 cloves
1 tablespoon ground coriander
2 teaspoons ground cumin
1 teaspoon ground white pepper
2 teaspoons ground cinnamon
1 teaspoon ground turmeric
1 teaspoon chili/chilli powder
½ nutmeg, finely grated

SERVES 4

First, make the curry powder. Using a mortar and pestle, finely grind the star anise, fennel seeds, and cloves. Mix these together with all the other curry powder spices. Set aside.

Peel and discard the tough outer casing of the lemon grass stalks. Finely chop the white bulbous part of the stalks, discarding the remainder.

Heat the oil in a flameproof casserole dish. Add in the onions, garlic, ginger, and lemon grass and fry gently, stirring, for 5 minutes until the onions have softened.

Mix the curry powder with 2–3 tablespoons of cold water to form a paste. Add the paste to the onion mixture and fry gently, stirring, for 3 minutes until fragrant. Add in the chicken thighs and coat in the paste. Add in the coconut milk, 100 ml/scant ½ cup of water, a little salt, the kaffir lime leaves, and cinnamon stick. Bring to the boil, reduce the heat, cover, and cook for 30 minutes.

Add in the new potatoes and cook, covered, for a further 30 minutes until the chicken is cooked through and the potatoes are tender. Serve with rice.

COCONUT & VANILLA CHICKEN CURRY

Coconut and vanilla make perfect partners, and here they combine with cashew nuts and an array of spices to make a chicken curry with an aromatic sauce and a real depth of flavor.

2 tablespoons vegetable or
   rapeseed oil
3½ lb./1.5 kg chicken pieces
1 onion, finely chopped
1 teaspoon Aromatic Sauce Mix
   (see below)
⅔ cup/150 ml chicken stock
1 teaspoon vanilla paste, or 1 vanilla
   bean/pod (seeds only)
⅓ cup/75 ml coconut milk
1 cup/125 g roasted cashew nuts,
   roughly chopped
cilantro/coriander, chopped,
   to garnish
basmati rice, to serve

AROMATIC SAUCE MIX
4 black peppercorns
4 cloves
1 star anise
½ teaspoon fennel seeds
3 dried red chiles/chillies
3 green cardamom pods
½ teaspoon poppy seeds
1 cinnamon stick
¼ teaspoon ground turmeric

SERVES 4

To make the aromatic sauce, heat a heavy-based skillet/frying pan and add the peppercorns, cloves, star anise, fennel seeds, chiles/chillies, cardamom, poppy seeds, and cinnamon. Roast for 1 minute. Tip into a mortar, add the turmeric, and grind to a powder using a pestle.

Heat the oil in a skillet/frying pan, add the chicken pieces, and lightly brown over a medium heat for 4–5 minutes. Set the chicken to one side, keeping it warm. Add the onion to the pan and cook through until translucent but not colored. Add a teaspoon of the aromatic sauce mix (reserve the rest for another time), stir well, and continue to cook for 2 minutes. Add the chicken stock, vanilla paste or seeds, and coconut milk and bring to a simmer. Add the set-aside chicken and cook for another 20–30 minutes.

Remove from the heat and strain the liquid. Combine the remaining liquid, chicken, and cashews in the pan and reheat. Serve with basmati rice, garnished with cilantro/coriander.

YUZU PAO CHICKEN WINGS

This Japanese spice mixture is hot and spicy, fragrant and delicious and lifts chicken wings to a new level. But be warned—this is a dish that will make your upper lip sweat and your eyes a little brighter!

2 tablespoons coriander seeds
½ teaspoon cumin seeds
½ teaspoon ground cinnamon
½ tablespoon salt
2 tablespoons olive oil
4 lb./1.8 kg chicken wings, halved
   at the joints, tips removed
½ cup/120 g red yuzu pao sauce
   (or sriracha sauce mixed with
   1 teaspoon yuzu juice or lemon
   juice)
3 tablespoons runny honey
3 tablespoons chopped fresh
   flat-leaf parsley
sugar snap peas/mangetout,
   to serve

SERVES 4–6

Toast the coriander and cumin seeds and the cinnamon in a small, dry pan over a medium heat until fragrant, then let cool. Use a mortar and pestle to grind the cooled spices to a fine powder.

Combine the spices, salt, and olive oil in a large bowl. Add the chicken wings and stir to coat, then cover and marinate in the fridge overnight or for at least 4 hours.

Preheat the oven to 375°F (190°C) Gas 5.

Spread the marinated wings on 2–3 baking sheets. Bake in the preheated oven for 50 minutes or until the wings are golden and the juices run clear when the thickest part is pierced to the bone. Set aside to cool slightly.

Combine the red yuzu pao sauce and the honey in a small bowl. Place the cooked wings in a large bowl, add the yuzu pao-honey mixture and half the parsley, then toss to coat. Serve garnished with the remaining parsley and with sugar snap peas/mangetout on the side.

BAKED PARMESAN WINGS

When baked, these wings have the flavor and crispiness of fried chicken, without the decadence of fried food. They are very versatile and can be enjoyed with a variety of dipping sauces.

⅓ cup/90 ml balsamic vinegar
¼ cup/50 g salt
1 bay leaf
1 teaspoon dried thyme
1 teaspoon dried oregano
1 teaspoon dried rosemary
4 lb./1.8 kg chicken wings, halved at the joints, tips removed
7 garlic cloves, finely chopped
3 tablespoons olive oil
1 tablespoon freshly ground black pepper
2 teaspoons hot red pepper/chilli flakes, or to taste
¼ cup/50 g fine breadcrumbs
1 cup/60 g finely grated Parmesan cheese

HOMEMADE KETCHUP

18 oz./500 g tomato paste/purée
½ cup/120ml white wine vinegar or apple cider vinegar
1 teaspoon garlic powder
1 tablespoon onion powder
2 tablespoons sugar
2 tablespoons molasses or treacle
1 teaspoon sea salt
1 teaspoon mustard powder
⅛ teaspoon each of ground cinnamon, cloves, allspice, and cayenne pepper
1 teaspoon powdered chia seeds, for thickness (optional)

SERVES 4-6

To make the ketchup, put all the ingredients in a blender or food processor with 1 cup/250 ml water and blend well. Chill in the fridge overnight or for at least 2 hours.

Preheat the oven to 450°F (230°C) Gas 7. Line 2–3 baking sheets with foil and grease with cooking spray or vegetable oil.

Combine the vinegar, salt, bay leaf, thyme, oregano, and rosemary with 6½ cups/1.5 litres water in a large saucepan and bring to a boil. Add the chicken wings, return to the boil, and cook for 15 minutes. Using a slotted spoon, transfer the wings to a cooling rack and allow to dry for 15 minutes.

Mash the garlic with a pinch of salt in a mortar and pestle until smooth. Add the olive oil, black pepper, and hot red pepper/chilli flakes and mix together, then transfer to a large bowl. Add the breadcrumbs, then the chicken wings and toss to coat. Sprinkle with half the cheese. Transfer to the prepared baking sheets and sprinkle with the remaining cheese.

Bake in the preheated oven for 20–25 minutes, until golden and the juices run clear when the thickest part is pierced to the bone.

CHICKEN TAGINE WITH HARISSA, ARTICHOKES & GREEN GRAPES

With the tangy notes of preserved lemon combined with the sweet grapes, this tagine is deliciously refreshing. It is best accompanied by buttery couscous or flatbread and a leafy salad. You can use ready-prepared artichoke hearts or bottoms, which are available canned or frozen.

4 chicken breasts, cut into thick
    strips or chunks
2 tablespoons olive oil
2 onions, halved lengthways and
    sliced with the grain
½ preserved lemon, thinly sliced
1–2 teaspoons sugar
1–2 teaspoons harissa (see page 76)
2 teaspoons tomato paste/purée
1¼ cups/300 ml chicken stock
    or water
14-oz./400-g can of artichoke hearts,
    drained, rinsed, and halved
about 16 fresh green grapes, halved
    lengthways
a bunch of fresh cilantro/coriander
    leaves, coarsely chopped
sea salt and freshly ground black
    pepper
flatbreads, to serve

MARINADE
2 garlic cloves
1 teaspoon ground turmeric
freshly squeezed juice of 1 lemon
1 tablespoon olive oil

SERVES 4–6

First, make the marinade. Crush the garlic cloves in a mortar and pestle, then add the turmeric, lemon juice, and olive oil and mix together. Tip into a large bowl and toss the chicken in the mixture, then cover and leave in the fridge to marinate for 1–2 hours.

Heat the oil in a tagine or a heavy-based casserole. Stir in the onions, preserved lemon, and sugar and sauté for 2–3 minutes, until slightly caramelized. Toss in the marinated chicken, then add the harissa and tomato paste/purée. Pour in the stock and bring to the boil. Reduce the heat, cover with a lid, and cook gently for 15 minutes.

Add in the artichoke hearts, cover with the lid again, and cook for a further 5 minutes. Add the grapes with some of the cilantro/coriander and season to taste with salt and pepper. Sprinkle with the remaining cilantro/coriander and serve accompanied by flatbreads to mop up the juices.

GRILLED HARISSA CHICKEN KABOBS

Spicy chicken, hot off the grill and served with lemon wedges and cracked green olives, is divine. Harissa is a fiery North African sauce—any leftover from this recipe can be stored in the fridge and used to flavor mayo, salad dressings, pastas, and grilled vegetables or spooned through rice dishes.

12 chicken thighs, skin on, boneless
¼ cup/60 ml honey
1 cup/225 g scratched green olives
lemon wedges, for squeezing
oil, for brushing the grate

HARISSA
2 dried Pasilla chiles/chillies
1 dried Ancho chile/chilli
1 roasted red (bell) pepper
2 fresh red Serrano chiles/chillies,
    roughly chopped
½ teaspoon coarse sea salt
4 garlic cloves
2 teaspoons ground cumin
1 teaspoon smoked paprika
2 tablespoons tomato paste/purée
2 tablespoons olive oil

SERVES 6–8

To make the harissa, place the dried chiles/chillies in a bowl, cover with boiling water, and soak for 30 minutes. Drain the chiles/chillies, reserving ¼ cup/60 ml of the soaking liquid.

Place the chiles/chillies, reserved liquid, and the remaining harissa ingredients in a mortar and pestle and blend to a rough paste.

Place the chicken thighs in a large ceramic dish. Mix together 4 tablespoons of harissa paste with the honey. Pour over the chicken and toss to coat completely. Cover and refrigerate for 6–24 hours.

Bring the chicken to room temperature and thread onto metal skewers. Heat the grill/barbecue to medium-high. Brush the grate with oil.

Place the skewers skin-side down on the grill and cook for 8 minutes until golden brown and crispy. Turn the skewers over and turn down the heat or move to a cooler part of the grill. Continue to cook for another 15 minutes. Check for doneness by inserting a sharp knife into the chicken to see that the meat is no longer pink and the juices run clear.

Remove the cooked skewers from the grill, cover, and rest for 5 minutes. To serve, pile on a plate and sprinkle with the olives and lemon wedges (if you wish, the lemon wedges can be briefly charred on the grill).

SEARED DUCK LAOS WITH
CUCUMBER NOODLE SALAD

Here the combination of seared duck and shredded cucumber tossed with rice noodles makes for a lovely lunch dish. Don't skimp on the marinating time, as this really adds to the depth of flavor.

9 oz./250 g duck breast fillet
9 oz./250 g dried rice vermicelli
   noodles
2 small cucumbers, deseeded
½ cup/75 g cherry tomatoes,
   quartered
2 red bird's eye chiles/chillies
1 garlic clove, roughly chopped
½ teaspoon salt
½ teaspoon granulated/caster sugar
freshly squeezed juice of ½ lime
2 teaspoons fish sauce
½ teaspoon shrimp paste

MARINADE
1 lemon grass stalk, trimmed
   and chopped
1 green chile/chilli, deseeded
   and chopped
2 garlic cloves, roughly chopped
a small bunch of fresh cilantro/
   coriander
2 tablespoons dark soy sauce
1 tablespoon fish sauce
2 teaspoons soft brown sugar

TO SERVE
toasted ground rice
chiles/chillies, sliced

SERVES 4

Start by marinating the duck. Score the duck through the skin and into the flesh with a sharp knife and place in a shallow dish. Blend the marinade ingredients together in a mortar and pestle until smooth, then smother the duck, rubbing well into the scores. Cover and place in the fridge for 4 hours.

Soak the noodles in a bowl of hot water for 20 minutes until softened. Drain well, shake dry, and set aside in a large mixing bowl.

Cut the cucumbers into batons and transfer to a large mixing bowl with the tomatoes.

Put the chiles/chillies and garlic in a mortar and pestle with the salt and sugar and pound to form a paste. Stir in the lime juice, fish sauce, and shrimp paste, then add to the cucumber mixture and stir well for several minutes until the cucumber is wilted.

Remove the duck from its marinade and cook on a preheated stovetop ridged grill pan (or heavy-based skillet/frying pan) for 4–5 minutes on each side. Remove from the pan and allow to rest for 5 minutes before slicing.

Arrange the noodles on a plate and spoon the cucumber salad in the middle. Top with the sliced, seared duck, garnished with toasted ground rice and red chiles/chillies.

QUAIL WITH BORLOTTI BEANS, BABY TOMATOES & SALMORIGLIO

Salmoriglio is a tangy southern Italian dressing or marinade made from lemon juice, olive oil, salt, and herbs. Here it works well with roasted quail.

1½ cups/300 g dried borlotti beans, soaked overnight (or fresh borlotti beans from their pods)
extra virgin olive oil
2 tablespoons red wine vinegar
6 garlic cloves, peeled
a few sprigs of fresh rosemary
20 baby plum tomatoes
1 teaspoon ground cumin
1 teaspoon ground coriander
½ teaspoon ground cinnamon
4 quail, rinsed and patted dry
sea salt and freshly ground black pepper

SALMORIGLIO
leaves from a handful of fresh marjoram or oregano
¼ teaspoon sea salt
freshly squeezed juice of ½ a lemon
4 tablespoons extra virgin olive oil

SERVES 4

If using dried beans, cover with three times their volume in water and soak overnight. Next day, refresh with clean water and place in a large ovenproof pot. If using fresh beans, start from this stage. Do not add salt to the beans as this will prevent them from softening. Bring almost to the boil, then reduce to a gentle simmer. Cook for 60-70 minutes or until almost tender (less for freshly podded, shelled beans).

Preheat the oven to 375°F (190°C) Gas 5. Drain most of the water from the beans, leaving about ⅓ cup/75 ml at the bottom. Add 1¾ cups/180 ml olive oil, the red wine vinegar, whole garlic cloves, rosemary, tomatoes, and 1 teaspoon sea salt. Cover tightly with kitchen foil and a lid, then place in the oven for 20-25 minutes until the beans and garlic are soft. Remove and let cool a little.

Increase the oven temperature to 400°F (200°C) Gas 6.

Mix together the cumin, coriander, cinnamon, 1 teaspoon sea salt, and ½ teaspoon ground black pepper. In a large bowl, rub the quail with a little olive oil, then sprinkle over the spice mix until the quail are well coated. Place on a baking sheet and roast for 20 minutes until golden and cooked through. Remove and leave to rest for 10 minutes.

Meanwhile, make the salmoriglio. Place the herbs in a mortar and pestle with the sea salt. Pound to a smooth paste. Add in a squeeze of lemon and slowly pour in the olive oil, stirring as you go with the pestle.

Spoon the beans, tomatoes, and garlic onto plates, place a quail on top, and drizzle over a little salmoriglio.

MEAT

STUFFED PORCHETTA

This traditional Italian dish is superb served with English mustard, fresh and pickled vegetables, and plenty of crusty bread.

4½ lb./2 kg boneless pork sirloin, butterflied and rind scored at ⅜-inch/1-cm intervals (your butcher may be able to do this for you)
2 cups plus 2 tablespoons/500 ml white wine
coarse sea salt and freshly ground black pepper

STUFFING
2 teaspoons fennel seeds
1 tablespoon extra virgin olive oil
4 garlic cloves, finely chopped
½ bunch of fresh flat-leaf parsley, finely chopped
2 tablespoons pine nuts
1 teaspoon hot red pepper/chilli flakes (optional)
1 teaspoon celery salt
grated zest of 1 lemon

TO SERVE
1 fennel bulb, shaved into thin slices
3 celery stalks and leaves
pickled vegetables
English mustard
crusty bread

cooking string

small roasting pan lined with baking parchment

SERVES 4–6

Place the pork, rind-side up, on a wire rack in the sink, and carefully pour boiling kettle water over the skin to help the score marks open, then leave to stand for 10 minutes to dry. Pat dry with paper towels.

Preheat the oven to 425°F (220°C) Gas 7.

Roast the fennel seeds in a dry pan for a few minutes, then crush using a mortar and pestle. Tip into a bowl and add all the other stuffing ingredients. Season to taste with salt and pepper.

Lay the pork out on a board, rind-side down, and rub the stuffing mixture over the flesh. Carefully roll up the sirloin widthways, then tie tightly with a piece of string in the middle. Tie at each end, about ½ inch/1 cm in, then at intervals along the length of the roll. If the stuffing escapes, push it back in.

Place the porchetta, skin-side up, in the lined roasting pan and pour the wine into the base. Season the rind generously with sea salt and roast in the preheated oven for about 35–40 minutes or until the skin starts to crackle and brown.

Reduce the oven temperature to 350°F (180°C) Gas 4 and roast for another 40 minutes until the pork is tender when pierced with a sharp knife. Cover and leave to rest for 20 minutes, then thinly slice and serve with a light salad of shaved fennel, celery stalks and leaves, pickled vegetables, English mustard, and crusty bread.

GOAN PORK VINDALOO

A vindaloo is essentially meat (traditionally pork) which has been cooked in vinegar and garlic, and this recipe combines these two ingredients with an array of different spices to create a melt-in-the-mouth dish with a real depth of flavor (don't be tempted to skimp on the marinating time.) A true vindaloo has Portuguese roots due to the 15th-century explorers who traveled from Europe to southern India and the name is dervied from the Portuguese *carne de vinha d'alhos* (which literally means "meat in garlic marinade".)

3 lb. 5 oz./1.5 kg pork shoulder, diced
2 tablespoons vegetable oil

MARINADE
10 dried Kashmiri chiles/chillies
1½ teaspoons cumin seeds
a ½-inch/1.5-cm piece of cassia bark
5 cloves
1 teaspoon coriander seeds
1 teaspoon black peppercorns
1 teaspoon ground turmeric
1 teaspoon salt
3 garlic cloves
3 tablespoons malt vinegar
4 tablespoons vegetable oil

CURRY SAUCE
5 tablespoons vegetable oil
1 teaspoon mustard seeds
1 teaspoon cumin seeds
a 1-inch/2.5-cm piece of fresh root
    ginger, thinly sliced
5 green chiles/chillies, slit
2 garlic cloves, thinly sliced
2 large onions, finely chopped
1 teaspoon salt
1 teaspoon ground cumin
1 teaspoon ground coriander
1 teaspoon ground turmeric
1 teaspoon paprika
1 teaspoon hot red pepper/
    chilli flakes
3 tablespoons tomato paste/purée
4 large tomatoes, chopped (core and
    seeds removed)
1 tablespoon granulated/caster sugar
1 tablespoon malt vinegar

TO SERVE
thinly sliced red onion
boiled rice or naan bread

SERVES 6

Start by making the marinade. In a skillet/frying pan, toast the Kashmiri chiles/chillies, cumin seeds, cassia bark, cloves, coriander seeds, and black peppercorns over a low-medium heat. Remove from the heat when the spices start to smell aromatic.

Grind the spices to a powder using a mortar and pestle. Add the remaining marinade ingredients to the ground spices and blend together to form a smooth paste.

Place the diced pork in a mixing bowl and add the marinade paste. Mix well so that the pork is coated all over. Allow the pork to marinate for a minimum of 2 hours or up to 24 hours in the fridge for a more intense flavor.

Once the meat has marinated, heat the 2 tablespoons of oil in a heavy-based pan until the oil is smoking. Add the pork in batches and seal all over; do not overcrowd the pan as you will cool down the temperature of the pan. When all of the pork is sealed, transfer to a baking sheet and set aside.

Add a splash of water to deglaze the pan and loosen all of the meat juices. Drain the flavored water into a measuring cup/jug and set aside as you will need it at a later stage.

For the curry sauce, heat the oil in the pan, add the mustard seeds and cook until they pop, then add the cumin seeds. When the cumin seeds have crackled, add the ginger, chiles/chillies, and garlic and stir in the hot oil for

1 minute. Add the onions and salt and stir well over a high heat to brown the onions. Once the onions have browned, reduce the heat and cover with a lid. Gently fry the onions until they have softened and browned. This should take 25–30 minutes, but the caramelized flavor will be worth it.

Once the onions have softened, add the ground cumin, coriander, turmeric, paprika, and hot red pepper/chilli flakes. Fry the spices for 1 minute to lose their raw aroma. Add the tomato paste/purée and fry for 2 minutes to cook away the sour acidic notes. Loosen the sauce by adding the reserved deglazing water.

Gently add the pork back into the pan and mix well. Pour in any juices left in the bottom of the baking sheet. Add 2 cups/ 500 ml water, stir well, cover with a lid, and simmer over low heat for 30 minutes.

Add the tomatoes, mix well, and cook for a further 30 minutes over a low heat with the lid on, stirring occasionally. When the tomatoes have nicely melted into the liquid to form a sauce, the curry is almost ready. Add the sugar and vinegar and cook for a further 5 minutes to let all of the flavors mingle.

Remove the pork from the heat, garnish with red onion, and serve with either rice or naan bread.

ITALIAN-STYLE ROAST PORK
WITH WHITE WINE, GARLIC & FENNEL

This is an excellent recipe for the weekend. You can leave it for hours, gently bubbling in the oven, and you will have a fantastic dish at the end of the day.

6½ lb./3 kg boneless, rolled pork butt/shoulder
2 tablespoons fennel seeds
1 tablespoon coarse sea salt
1 teaspoon black peppercorns
1 teaspoon crushed dried chiles/chillies
6 large garlic cloves, roughly chopped
freshly squeezed juice of 2 lemons
2 tablespoons olive oil
¾ cup/175 ml dry white wine

large roasting pan with a rack

ovenproof dish

SERVES 8

Preheat the oven to 400°F (200°C) Gas 6.

Cut deep slits in the pork skin with a sharp knife. Grind the fennel seeds, salt, peppercorns, and chiles/chillies using a mortar and pestle. Add the chopped garlic and pound to a rough paste. Using your hands, smother the paste all over the pork, working it into the slits.

Put the pork on a wire rack and place it over a roasting pan. Cook, skin-side up in the preheated oven for 25–30 minutes. Remove from the oven and reduce the heat to 250°F (120°C) Gas ½. Turn the pork over and pour half the lemon juice and all the olive oil over it. Return the pork to the oven and cook for at least 7 hours, checking it every couple of hours—it should be sizzling quietly. Ovens vary, so you may want to increase the temperature slightly.

About halfway through the cooking time, spoon off the excess fat and squeeze the remaining lemon juice over the meat. About 30 minutes before the pork is due to be cooked, remove it from the oven and increase the heat to 425°F (220°C) Gas 7. Transfer the pork, skin-side up, to a clean ovenproof dish and, when the oven is hot, return the pork to the oven for about 15 minutes to crisp up the crackling. Remove from the oven and let rest.

Pour off any excess fat from the original roasting pan and add the wine and ¾ cup/175 ml water. Simmer gently on the top of the stove for 10 minutes, scraping up any sticky burnt-on bits from the edges of the pan. Strain the juices through a strainer/sieve and keep warm. Carve the pork into thick slices and serve with some of the pan juices poured over.

SPICED PULLED PORK HASH

Mix roasted sweet potatoes and melt-in-the-mouth pulled pork for a tasty take on hash. The spicy mix of seasoning and the tender pulled pork will melt in your mouth. The pork will take 4–5 hours to cook, so you need to start this recipe in the morning or cook the pork the day before.

14 oz./400 g sweet potatoes, peeled
2 tablespoons vegetable oil
2 tablespoons butter
1 red onion, chopped
⅛–¼ teaspoon cayenne pepper,
    to taste
salt and freshly ground black pepper

PULLED PORK
1½ lb./700 g boneless pork butt/
    shoulder
1 tablespoon caraway seeds
2 whole cloves
1 star anise
½ tablespoon whole black
    peppercorns
½ cup/100 g coarse sea salt

SERVES 4

Preheat the oven to 250°F (120°C) Gas 4.

First, prepare the pulled pork. Combine the caraway seeds, cloves, star anise, and peppercorns in a mortar and grind with a pestle. Crush until ground to the same texture as the coarse salt. Mix the ground spices with the salt. Firmly rub the spice rub into the pork until it is all used up and the meat is completely covered. Place the pork in a roasting pan and cover tightly with kitchen foil.

Cook in the preheated oven for 4–5 hours, turning once or twice during this time. When ready, the meat will be tender enough for you to pull it into shreds using two forks.

Meanwhile, cut the sweet potatoes into small ¼-inch/ 0.5-cm cubes. Heat the oil in a skillet/frying pan and when hot, add the sweet potato cubes. Stir-fry for about 10 minutes until cooked through. Set aside until needed.

When you are ready to cook the hash, melt the butter in a skillet/frying pan over a medium heat. Add the onion and cook for about 2 minutes until slightly softened. Add the shredded spicy pork and continue to cook for 2 minutes more.

Stir the cooked sweet potatoes into the pork and onion mixture and toss. Cook, stirring occasionally, for about 5 minutes, until everything is piping hot. Season to taste with salt, black pepper, and cayenne pepper and serve immediately.

SLOW-ROASTED LEG OF LAMB

Marinate the lamb overnight to allow the flavors to penetrate the meat. As the joint roasts, it releases its own liquor which acts as a lip-smackingly good gravy, and the marinade cooks to form a delicious cross between a cooked rub and a glaze.

3½–4 lb./1.5–1.7 kg leg of lamb, on the bone

PASTE (MAKES 2½ CUPS/625 G)
7 oz./200 g. (about 6) green chiles/chillies
7 oz./200 g (about 40) garlic cloves
7 oz./200 g (about 8 x 2-inch/5-cm pieces) fresh root ginger
3½ tablespoons vegetable oil
1 tablespoon salt

MARINADE
2 teaspoons coriander seeds
2 teaspoons cumin seeds
8 tablespoons vegetable oil
3 teaspoons salt
1 teaspoon black peppercorns
1 teaspoon hot red pepper/chilli flakes
1 teaspoon ground turmeric
1 teaspoon tandoori powder
1 teaspoon gram/chickpea flour
3 large sprigs of mint
2 teaspoons paste (see above recipe)
a small bunch of cilantro/coriander (with stalks)
5 garlic cloves
3 tablespoons plain/natural yogurt
freshly squeezed juice of 1 lemon

GRAVY
3 onions, thinly sliced
2 tablespoons all-purpose/plain flour

SERVES 6

Make the paste by blitzing together the ingredients in a food processor to form a coarse paste. (Leftover paste can be stored in the fridge for up to 2 weeks.)

Next, make the marinade. Toast the coriander and cumin seeds in a dry skillet/frying pan until aromatic. Blend all of the marinade ingredients, including the toasted seeds, together using a mortar and pestle to make a paste.

Using a sharp knife, make deep incisions across the lamb and rub the paste all over and into the deep cuts. Leave to marinate for 24 hours in the fridge on a lined baking sheet. (Sometimes acid in a marinade can react with certain metals, which may cause your meat to pick up an unpleasant flavor, so it is best to protect your meat by lining the baking sheet.)

Preheat the oven to 350°F (180°C) Gas 4.

Scrape off as much of the marinade as you can and reserve to be used later. Seal and brown the joint all over in a pan. Set aside.

For the gravy, put the onions in a roasting pan, add 1 cup/250 ml water, and sprinkle over the flour. Place the sealed lamb on top and roast in the preheated oven for 30 minutes. Cover the pan tightly with foil, reduce the oven temperature to 300°F (150°C) Gas 2, and allow the joint to slow-roast for 3½ hours.

Remove the joint from the oven and leave to rest, covered, for 15 minutes before serving. The joint must be tender, so that the meat effortlessly falls off the bone when carved.

BAKED LAMB TAGINE WITH
QUINCES, FIGS & HONEY

This shoulder of lamb is marinated in chermoula (a Moroccan herb and spice mix) and baked slowly. If you wish, use apples or pears instead of quinces.

3¼ lb./1.5 kg shoulder of lamb, on the bone
2 tablespoons ghee
2 red onions, cut into wedges
225 g/1¾ cups ready-to-eat prunes, pitted
1¾ cups/225 g ready-to-eat dried figs, or fresh figs, halved
3 tablespoons/40 g butter
2 fresh quinces, quartered and cored (soak in water with a squeeze of lemon juice until ready to use)
2 tablespoons orange blossom water
2 tablespoons dark, runny honey
a bunch each of flat-leaf parsley and cilantro/coriander, chopped

CHERMOULA
4 garlic cloves, chopped
a 2-inch/5-cm piece of fresh ginger, peeled and chopped
1 red chile/chilli, deseeded and chopped
1 teaspoon sea salt
a small bunch each of cilantro/coriander and flat-leaf parsley, chopped
2–3 teaspoons ground coriander
2–3 teaspoons ground cumin
3 tablespoons olive oil
2 tablespoons dark, runny honey
freshly squeezed juice of 1 lemon

SERVES 4–6

First, make the chermoula. Using a mortar and pestle, pound the garlic, ginger, chile/chilli, and salt to form a coarse paste. Add the fresh cilantro/coriander and parsley and pound into the paste. Beat in the ground coriander and cumin, and bind with the olive oil, honey, and lemon juice. Cut small incisions in the shoulder of lamb with a sharp knife and rub the chermoula well into the meat. Cover and leave in the fridge for at least 6 hours, or overnight.

Preheat the oven to 350°F (180°C) Gas 4.

Heat the ghee in a tagine or a heavy-based casserole, add the lamb and brown it all over. Transfer the meat to a plate. Stir the onions and any leftover chermoula into the ghee. Add the prunes and if using dried figs, add them at this stage. Pour in 1¼ cups/300 ml water and put the lamb back into the tagine. Cover with the lid and put the tagine in the oven for about 2 hours.

Towards the end of the cooking time, melt the butter in a heavy-based pan, toss in the quince and sauté until golden brown. Remove the tagine from the oven and place the quince around the meat (if using fresh figs, add them at this stage). Splash the orange blossom water over the lamb and drizzle the honey over the meat and the fruit. Return the tagine to the oven for a further 25–30 minutes, until the meat and fruit are nicely browned and the lamb is so tender it almost falls off the bone. Sprinkle the chopped parsley and cilantro/coriander over the top and serve immediately.

INDIAN-SPICED LEG OF
LAMB COOKED IN A SALT CRUST

This is a simple way to cook lamb—coat it in a thick crust and roast it in the oven. The aromas from the spices are intoxicating, especially the fresh curry leaves hidden in the crust. Serve with a refreshing raita on the side.

3 lb./1.3 kg leg of lamb, on the bone
4 garlic cloves, sliced

SPICE RUB
20 green cardamom pods, bashed
1 teaspoon cumin seeds
1 cinnamon stick, broken into pieces
½ teaspoon each of whole cloves, turmeric, chipotle powder, and Spanish smoked paprika
2 tablespoons olive oil

SALT CRUST
2½ cups/550 g coarse sea salt
3½ cups/450 g all-purpose/plain flour
small bunch of fresh curry leaves

RAITA
2 garlic cloves
225 ml/1 cup plain/natural yogurt
1 small cucumber, grated
2 tablespoons fresh mint leaves, torn
sea salt, to season
ground sumac, to sprinkle

SERVES 6-8

Using a sharp knife, stab the lamb all over and stud with the slices of garlic. Set aside.

To make the spice rub, put all the dry ingredients in a skillet/frying pan and dry roast over a low heat, stirring continuously until they are lightly toasted. Pound the toasted spices to a rough mixture using a mortar and pestle. Add the olive oil and stir to a paste. Spread the paste all over the lamb and chill in the fridge for at least 2 hours or for up to 24 hours (if refrigerated overnight, remove 1 hour before cooking).

Preheat the oven to 400°F (200°C) Gas 6.

To make the salt crust, mix the salt, flour, and curry leaves together in a bowl with 1 cup/250 ml water to give a doughy consistency. If the mixture is too dry, add more water 1 tablespoon at a time. Roll out on a floured worktop to twice the size of the lamb. Put the lamb leg at one end of the pastry and fold over the remaining dough. Seal, making sure there are no holes for any steam to escape. Put in a lightly oiled roasting pan and bake in the preheated oven for 1 hour. Remove the lamb from the oven and let it rest for 10-15 minutes.

For the raita, crush the garlic in a mortar and pestle. Mix with the yogurt, cucumber, and mint. Season with sea salt and sprinkle with sumac.

Peel off the crust and place the lamb on a large board to carve. Serve with raita on the side.

PULLED LAMB SHOULDER
WITH ORANGE & CINNAMON PILAF

Slow and steady wins the race, and this lamb dish does just that, languishing in a low oven for hours, enshrouded in herbs and spices, until finally, it admits defeat and collapses at the merest touch.

3¼ lb./1.5 kg lamb shoulder, most of the surface fat cut off
olive oil
1¼ cups/300 ml chicken stock
1 scant cup/200 ml white wine (or replace with more chicken stock)

MARINADE
2 teaspoons coriander seeds
2 teaspoons cumin seeds
a handful of fresh mint leaves
zest and juice of 1 orange
4 garlic cloves, crushed
2 teaspoons ground cinnamon
sea salt and freshly ground black pepper

PILAF
1½ cups/300 g basmati rice
extra virgin olive oil
1 large onion, chopped
1 teaspoon cumin seeds
1 cinnamon stick
1 orange
⅔ cup/100 g pine nuts, lightly roasted until golden
½ cup/80 g raisins

TO SERVE
1 cup/250 g soy or Greek yogurt
1–2 fronds of fresh dill, chopped
1 pomegranate, seeds removed

SERVES 4–6

First, make the marinade. Place the coriander and cumin seeds in a dry skillet/frying pan over a medium heat for about 3 minutes. Next, pound them using a mortar and pestle. Finely chop ⅔ of the mint and add this to a bowl with the orange zest and juice. Add the ground coriander and cumin, garlic, cinnamon, and 1 teaspoon of salt and pepper and combine together.

Make incisions all over the lamb and place in a large roasting tray; cover with the marinade and massage into the flesh. Cover and set aside for 1 hour, or in the fridge overnight (if refrigerated overnight, remove 1 hour before cooking).

Preheat the oven to 320°F (160°C) Gas 3.

Drizzle a little olive oil over the lamb, pour the stock and white wine into the tray, and cover very tightly with two layers of kitchen foil. Place in the center of the oven for 5 hours.

Remove and leave to stand for at least 15 minutes, covered in the foil.

To make the pilaf, rinse the rice well until the water runs clear. Add into a pot of boiling salted water, and return to the boil for exactly 6 minutes. Drain very well.

Place 2 tablespoons oil in a skillet/frying pan (with a tightly fitting lid) over a medium heat. Add the onion, cumin seeds, and cinnamon stick and cook for 10 minutes until the onions have softened. Peel 4 strips of zest from the orange and add to the skillet/pan with most of the pine nuts, turn up the heat, and cook on high for 1 minute, stirring constantly.

Remove the onion and spice mix to a plate. Place the same skillet/pan on a medium heat and add 3 tablespoons olive oil and 2 tablespoons water.

When hot, spoon in a thin layer of rice across the base of the skillet/pan. Stir the raisins and the onion and spice mix into the remaining rice, then spoon that on top of the base of rice, being careful not to squash it down. Using the handle of a wooden spoon, poke some holes in the rice so the steam can escape. Wrap the lid in a clean dish towel and cover.

Leave the skillet/pan on a medium heat for 2 minutes, then reduce to the

gentlest heat possible and cook for 30 minutes, without removing the lid.

Fill the kitchen sink ¼ full with cold water. When the rice is done, sit the pan straight into the water and leave for a few minutes. Invert the rice onto a serving platter.

Combine the yogurt and dill with a pinch of salt. Serve the lamb, pulled into chunks, with the pilaf alongside. Dollop over the dill yogurt and scatter the pomegranate seeds and remaining mint and pine nuts over the top.

BEEF TRI-TIP POKE

This Californian poke dish uses tri-tip beef (a cut from the bottom sirloin), but you can substitute topside (preferably the corner cut) or bavette/goose skirt.

3 lb. 5 oz./1.5 kg beef tri-tip or topside corner cut, or bavette/goose skirt

DRY RUB
1 tablespoon cumin seeds
1 tablespoon coriander seeds
1 teaspoon smoked paprika
1½ tablespoons salt

PINTO BEANS
3 slices/rashers smoked streaky bacon, chopped
5½ oz./150 g smoked cooked ham, diced
14-oz./400-g can chopped tomatoes
3 garlic cloves, chopped
2 teaspoons dark soy sauce
2 teaspoons ketjap manis (Indonesian soy sauce)
1 teaspoon chipotle paste
1 teaspoon smoked paprika
14-oz./400-g can pinto beans (or black beans), drained and rinsed

TO SERVE
9 oz./250 g kale, finely chopped
Red Salsa (see page 19) or ketchup (see page 46)

SERVES 6

For the dry rub, heat a dry skillet/frying pan and lightly toast the cumin and coriander seeds. When slightly colored, grind to a coarse powder using a mortar and pestle. Add the smoked paprika and salt. Rub the mixture all over the meat.

To oven roast tri-tip/topside, preheat the oven to 425°F (220°C) Gas 7. Place the beef in a roasting pan and roast for 15 minutes to seal the surfaces, then loosely cover with foil and reduce the heat to 350°F (180°C) Gas 4 for 30 minutes or until the inside is medium-rare. Baste occasionally with pan juices. At the end of the cooking time, remove the foil and turn the heat right up to brown.

To cook bavette/goose skirt in a ridged pan, lightly oil the meat. Heat the pan to very hot, add the meat, leave for 3 minutes, then turn over for 3 minutes. Turn again but at right angles for another 3 minutes, then turn again at right angles for a final 3 minutes. This should give you a rare to medium-rare result. Leave a little longer if undercooked.

Make up the pinto beans. Heat up a large skillet/frying pan and add the bacon and diced ham. When browned, add the remaining ingredients apart from the beans. Turn down the heat and simmer for 20 minutes. Add the beans and 2 cups/500 ml water, and simmer for another 20 minutes.

To serve, dice the meat into ½-inch/1-cm cubes. Place some kale in bowls, followed by the pinto beans and beef. Top with Red Salsa or ketchup.

PEPPER-CRUSTED STEAKS
WITH RED WINE SAUCE

This has to be the ultimate fast-food recipe—you can make it from start to finish in just 5 minutes. The red wine gives a wonderful instant sauce that takes the dish into the luxury league. After you have made this a couple of times, you'll find you won't need measurements—just pour in a dash of brandy, half a glass of red wine, and a slosh of cream to finish, and away you go.

1 tablespoon mixed peppercorns
½ teaspoon sea salt
1 teaspoon all-purpose/plain flour
2 thinly cut rump steaks, 4¼–5½ oz./
   125–150 g each, fat removed
1 tablespoon olive oil
1½ tablespoons/25 g butter
2 tablespoons brandy
⅓ cup/75 ml full-bodied fruity
   red wine
3 tablespoons fresh beef or chicken
   stock
1 teaspoon redcurrant jelly or a few
   drops of balsamic vinegar
   (optional)
2 tablespoons sour cream/
   crème fraîche

TO SERVE
arugula/rocket salad
crusty bread
garlic mash or fries/chips (see
   page 29)

SERVES 2

Put the peppercorns and salt in a mortar and pound with a pestle until coarsely ground. Tip into a shallow dish and mix in the flour. Dip each steak into the pepper mixture and press the coating in lightly, turning to coat both sides.

Heat a skillet/frying pan over a medium heat and add the oil and the butter. Once the butter has melted, add the steaks to the pan and cook for 1½ minutes. Turn them over and cook for 30 seconds on the other side. Transfer the steaks to 2 warm plates.

Pour the brandy into the pan and light it carefully with a long cook's match or taper. When the flames die down, add the wine and cook for a few seconds.

Add the stock and simmer for 1–2 minutes. Sweeten with a little redcurrant jelly or balsamic vinegar, if you like, then stir in the sour cream/ crème fraîche.

Pour the sauce over the steaks and serve with an arugula/rocket salad and some crusty bread. If you're not in a hurry, this also goes really well with garlic mash or fries/chips.

UMAMI STEAK TAGLIATA

This rub is a beautiful thing, but with good-quality steak and a drizzle of green extra virgin olive oil, it is ridiculously sublime. For extra umami add a couple of Portobello mushrooms to the dish—just sprinkle them with a little rub and pan-fry them with the steaks. This rub recipe makes more than you need for 2 steaks but you can store the excess in a tightly sealed jar and use on other meats and fish.

2 steaks (rib-eye, New York strip/
    sirloin, or filet mignon/fillet)
extra virgin olive oil, for drizzling

GARLIC PESTO
2 large garlic cloves
leaves from 2 sprigs of rosemary
5 black peppercorns
a good pinch of salt
extra virgin olive oil

UMAMI RUB (MAKES 4 OZ./120 G)
1 tablespoon dried mushrooms
    (shiitake, porcini, or a mix; you
    will need about a handful to make
    a tablespoon)
2 tablespoons sea salt
1 tablespoon brown sugar
1 tablespoon smoked paprika
1 tablespoon dried oregano
2 teaspoons ground cumin
2 teaspoons garlic powder
1 teaspoon ground black pepper
½ teaspoon cayenne pepper
    (or to taste)

SERVES 2

Using a mortar and pestle, pound together the garlic, rosemary, black peppercorns, and salt to a chunky pesto consistency. Add just enough olive oil to form a loose pesto and set aside.

Next make the rub. Start by grinding the dried mushrooms to a powder in the mortar and pestle. Tip into a bowl with all the other rub ingredients in a bowl and mix together well.

Generously rub each steak all over with about a tablespoon of the rub. Once they are well coated, place the steaks on a plate and drizzle with some of the garlic pesto, keeping the rest aside. If time permits, cover the steaks in plastic wrap/clingfilm and leave them for about 20–30 minutes to come to room temperature.

Preheat a skillet/frying pan on a medium-high heat. Once hot, cook the steaks to your liking.

Once cooked, remove the steaks from the pan and leave to rest for a minute or so in a warm place. Slice diagonally with a sharp knife.

Serve on warmed plates topped with any pan juices, an extra spoonful of the garlic pesto, and a good drizzle of extra virgin olive oil.

CHIANG MAI BEEF NOODLE CURRY

As the name suggests, this dish originates from Chiang Mai in the north of Thailand. It can be served as a soup or a stew-like dish of noodles with a curried coconut sauce.

2 red Asian shallots, chopped
1 garlic clove, roughly chopped
½-inch/1-cm piece of fresh turmeric
   (or ½ teaspoon ground turmeric)
a pinch of salt
1 tablespoon Thai red curry paste
⅓ cup/100 ml coconut cream
2 tablespoons grated palm sugar
1 tablespoon fish sauce
2 teaspoons dark soy sauce
2½ cups/600 ml chicken stock
4 kaffir lime leaves, pounded
9 oz./250 g thinly sliced beef fillet
2 tablespoons chopped fresh
   cilantro/coriander
1 lb./500 g fresh egg noodles
vegetable oil, for deep frying

TO SERVE
scallions/spring onions, shredded
deep-fried shallots
1 lime, cut into wedges

SERVES 4

Put the shallots, garlic, turmeric, and salt in a mortar and pestle and pound until fairly smooth. Stir in the red curry paste.

Add the coconut cream to a wok set over a medium heat and cook for about 3 minutes until the cream bubbles and splits. Stir in curry paste mixture and continue to cook for a further 2 minutes. Stir in the palm sugar, fish sauce, and soy sauce, and bring to the boil. Add the chicken stock and lime leaves and simmer gently for 15 minutes.

Meanwhile, pour vegetable oil into a wok or large saucepan to reach about 2 inches/5 cm up the side of the pan and set over a medium heat. Test the temperature of the pan by dropping a cube of bread into the hot oil—it should crisp within 30 seconds. Carefully add 2 oz./50 g of the noodles and deep-fry (be careful as the oil will spit) until crisp. Drain on paper towels and set aside to garnish.

Cook the remaining noodles by plunging them into a large saucepan of boiling water. Return to the boil and cook for 2–3 minutes until al dente. Drain well and divide between warmed bowls.

Stir the beef and cilantro/coriander into the wok with the curry mixture and immediately remove the pan from the heat.

Spoon the curried beef and sauce over the noodles and serve with the deep-fried noodles, scallions/spring onions, deep-fried shallots, and lime wedges.

FISH & SEAFOOD

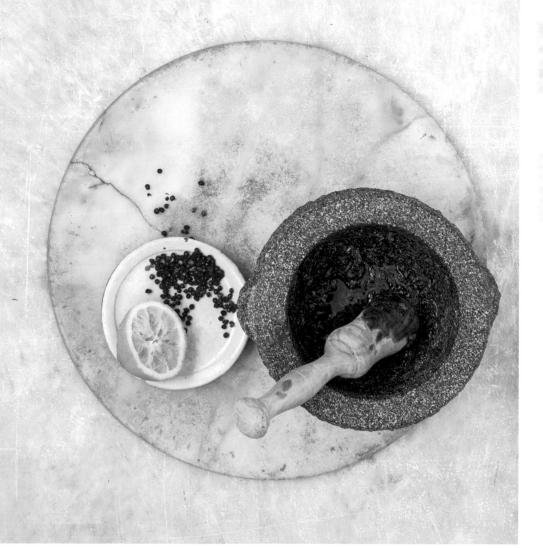

SALT-CURED GRAVADLAX WITH CAPER SAUCE

It seems everyone has a favorite way of making this classic dish. This overnight version is quick compared with the traditional method of curing for several days. Wild salmon makes a huge difference; if it's not available, use organic farmed salmon. The gravadlax will keep for 5 days in the fridge.

2½ lb./1.1 kg wild salmon fillet, boned and with skin on (this is one side of a whole salmon)
2 tablespoons juniper berries
2 tablespoons black peppercorns
1 cup/110 g coarse sea salt
½ cup/225 g brown sugar
3 bunches of fresh dill
¼ cup/60 ml gin
lemon wedges and baguette slices, to serve

CAPER SAUCE
2 tablespoons salt
2 tablespoons cornichons
1 tablespoon salted capers
1 cup/225 g sour cream/ crème fraîche
finely grated zest and freshly squeezed juice of 1 lemon

a prepared baking sheet or dish

SERVES 8

You will need a baking sheet or shallow dish that will accommodate the whole salmon. Line the bottom of this with plastic wrap/clingfilm.

Crush the juniper berries and black peppercorns using a mortar and pestle. Tip into a bowl and mix with the sea salt and brown sugar.

Sprinkle half the salt mixture on top of the prepared baking sheet or dish and spread one of the bunches of dill over the salt mixture. Place the salmon, skin-side down on top of the dill and drizzle with the gin. Cover the salmon with the remainder of the salt mixture and then top with the remaining dill.

Cover the salmon with plastic wrap/clingfilm, making sure it is airtight. Next, you need to put a weight on the salmon; a heavy saucepan or pizza stone is ideal. Put the salmon in the fridge overnight to cure for 12 hours.

To make the caper sauce, crush the salt, cornichons, and capers using a mortar and pestle. Mix in the remaining ingredients and transfer to a serving bowl, cover, and refrigerate.

Unwrap the salmon and remove the dill. Place the salmon on a wooden board. Using the back of a knife, scrape off the salt mixture.

To serve, cut the salmon as thinly as possible in diagonal slices. Serve with the caper sauce, lemon wedges, and a crusty baguette.

FISH TACOS

A great fish taco depends on the freshness of the fish, the quality of the tortilla, and the punchiness of the salsas, contrasted against the creaminess of the crema and the crunchiness of the slaw. Use white fish fillets such as pollock, hake, or snapper and coat in a spicy mix of cumin, coriander, and paprika.

1 tablespoon cumin seeds
1 tablespoon coriander seeds
1 teaspoon smoked paprika
½ teaspoon salt
1¾ lb./800 g white fish fillets, such as pollock, hake, snapper, or any easy-to-fillet flat fish
flour, for dusting
salt and freshly ground black pepper
2 tablespoons vegetable oil

CREMA
2 tablespoons mayonnaise
4 tablespoons Greek-style yogurt
1 teaspoon Red Salsa (see page 19) or Tabasco sauce

SLAW
14 oz./400 g white cabbage, coarsely shredded
1 carrot, coarsely grated
½ onion, thinly sliced

TO SERVE
8 small corn or flour tortillas
1 ripe avocado, peeled, pitted/stoned, and sliced
1 lime, sliced
1 cucumber, thinly sliced

SERVES 4

Make up the crema by mixing together the mayonnaise, yogurt, and the Salsa or Tabasco. Set aside.

Combine the cabbage, carrot, and onion into a slaw. Set aside.

Heat a small, dry skillet/frying pan and lightly toast the cumin and coriander seeds. When slightly colored, grind to a coarse powder using a mortar and pestle. Mix in the smoked paprika and salt. Rub this mixture all over the fish fillets and set aside for at least 30 minutes.

Prepare the fish by slicing it into manageable portions for 8 tacos, then dust in flour combined with a little salt and pepper. Heat the oil in a skillet/frying pan and fry the fish in two batches until just slightly browned and cooked through. Transfer to a plate lined with paper towels to drain, then keep warm.

Heat a cast iron pan to warm the tortillas until slightly charred and warmed through.

To make up the tacos, place some of the slaw on each tortilla, add the fish, and drizzle over the crema. Serve with slices of avocado, lime, and cucumber.

HOT & SOUR FISH SOUP

This soup from Laos combines sweet, sour, and salty all in one colorful bowl, and as you simmer the stock, it becomes increasingly fragrant. If you want to turn up the heat, add a few dashes of sriracha sauce.

9 oz./200 g cellophane noodles
6 kaffir lime leaves, torn
1 large red chile/chilli, roughly chopped
1-inch/2.5-cm piece of fresh ginger, peeled and chopped
1 lemon grass stalk, trimmed and roughly chopped
2 garlic cloves
2½ pints/1.5 litres chicken stock
2 shallots, finely chopped
1 lb./500 g fish steaks or fillets, such as striped bass or bream
1 cup/50 g spinach, torn
4 tablespoons roasted sun-blush tomatoes, chopped
freshly squeezed juice of 1 lime
2 tablespoons fish sauce
a few dashes of sriracha (optional)
a bunch of fresh cilantro/coriander, roughly chopped

SERVES 4

Soak the noodles in a bowl of hot water for 10 minutes until softened. Drain well, shake dry, and set aside.

Put the lime leaves, chile/chilli, ginger, lemon grass, and garlic in a mortar and pestle and pound together until fragrant—it should still be quite bitty. Transfer this paste to a saucepan set over a medium heat and pour over the stock. Bring to the boil, then simmer gently for 20 minutes until really aromatic.

Add the shallots to the pan and simmer for 5 minutes, then carefully add the fish fillets to the pan and cook gently for 4–5 minutes until cooked through. Remove the pan from the heat and stir in the spinach, sun-blush tomatoes, lime juice, fish sauce, sriracha, if using, and cilantro/coriander. Cover with a lid and set aside for 5 minutes to allow the flavors to develop.

Divide the noodles between bowls and carefully spoon the fish on top. Pour over the soup and serve at once.

PASTA WITH SARDINES

This is a classic Sicilian pasta dish, but you'll find many recipe variations. This version includes fennel, anchovies, and raisins, and definitely falls into the category of comfort food .

12½ oz./350 g dried spaghetti
fennel fronds, to garnish
2 tablespoons extra virgin olive oil, not too strong

PANGRATTATO
1 garlic clove, finely chopped
1 tablespoon olive oil
5¼ oz./150 g open-textured, crustless sourdough-type bread, blitzed into breadcumbs
sea salt and freshly ground black pepper

SAUCE
1 tablespoon olive oil
¾ cup/50 g pine nuts
1 garlic clove, finely chopped
1 large fennel bulb (reserve the fronds), finely sliced
1 onion, chopped
7 tablespoons/100 ml dry white wine
6 butterflied sardines, pin boned
6 anchovies in oil
⅓ cup/50 g dark raisins

SERVES 4

Preheat the oven to 350°F (180°C) Gas 4.

To make the pangrattato, pound the garlic with the olive oil, salt, and pepper in a mortar and pestle. Stir in the breadcrumbs, then tip the mixture onto a parchment-lined baking sheet. Bake in the preheated oven for approximately 6 minutes, stirring occasionally, until golden. Allow to cool, then pound until fine using a mortar and pestle.

To make the sauce, heat the olive oil in a large skillet/ frying pan, add the pine nuts, and stir until golden. Add the garlic, fennel, and onion and cook until tender. Add the wine, sardines, anchovies, and raisins and simmer for 8 minutes on a low heat.

Cook the spaghetti in rolling boiling salted water and drain, reserving a little of the water to slacken the sardine sauce.

Mix the pasta and sardines together, and scatter generously with the breadcrumbs and fennel fronds. Drizzle with the olive oil and serve immediately.

SMOKED MACKEREL WITH PINK
PEPPER & SQUID INK SPAGHETTI

This warm salad has it all—dramatic colors and amazing flavor combinations.

2 teaspoons pink peppercorns
a handful of fresh flat-leaf parsley,
　finely chopped
½ teaspoon sea salt flakes
¼ teaspoon freshly ground black
　pepper
4 tablespoons extra virgin olive oil,
　plus extra if needed
freshly squeezed juice of ½ lemon
7 oz./200 g dried squid ink pasta or
　5½ oz./160 g fresh squid ink pasta
7 oz./200 g smoked mackerel fillets
1 large fennel bulb, thinly sliced
1 orange, zested, peeled, and
　segmented
a handful of fresh dill, chopped

SERVES 2

Grind the pink peppercorns, parsley, salt, black pepper, and oil in a mortar and pestle until the peppercorns are crushed. Add the lemon juice to make a loose pesto-like dressing. Set aside.

Put a large pan of salted water on to boil for the pasta. Add the pasta to the salted boiling water and stir with a long carving fork to stop it sticking together. Bring the water back up to the boil, then lower the heat slightly and cook as directed on the packet. Only partially cover with a lid to allow some of the steam to escape, as fully covering will cause the pasta to stew.

Meanwhile, flake the mackerel into chunks and place in a serving dish. Add the peppercorn dressing mixture, fennel, orange zest and segments, and dill.

Test the pasta to make sure it is cooked and drain, but keep a cup of the cooking water.

Tip the hot drained pasta into the mackerel mixture, add a small splash of the retained pasta water and a little more olive oil if necessary. Toss well until the pasta is coated with the dressing. Season to taste and serve immediately.

SPICE-CRUSTED SEA BASS
WITH MANGO SALSA

This is a very quick dish to make, but really full of flavor due to the spice crust and fresh mango salsa. Feel free to use whatever spices you have to hand—fennel seeds and mustard seeds also work particularly well with the sea bass.

1 tablespoon coriander seeds
1 tablespoon cumin seeds
2 teaspoons caraway seeds
½ teaspoon sweet/smoked paprika
1 egg white
4 x 6-oz./180-g sea bass fillets
sea salt and freshly ground black
    pepper

MANGO SALSA
1 mango, not too ripe or soft
½ a red onion, about 1 oz./35 g, very
    finely chopped
1 fresh red chile/chilli, deseeded and
    very finely chopped
zest of 1 lime, freshly squeezed juice
    of ½, and 4 wedges to serve
a small handful of fresh mint leaves,
    chopped

SERVES 4

Using a mortar and pestle, roughly pound the coriander, cumin, and caraway seeds with ½ teaspoon sea salt and ½ teaspoon black pepper. When roughly ground with little bits of whole seeds remaining, add in the smoked paprika and combine.

Whisk the egg white in a wide flat bowl. Coat the sea bass fillets one at a time with the egg white, then evenly sprinkle the ground spice mix over both sides of the fish.

To make the salsa, peel the mango, remove the pit/stone, and dice the flesh. Place in a bowl and combine with the red onion, chile/chilli, lime zest and juice, and mint. Season to taste with a little sea salt and pepper.

Pour 2 teaspoons olive oil into a wide skillet/frying pan over a high heat, and when hot, fry the sea bass for 2–3 minutes on both sides. If you can't fit all of them in at once, fry in batches, as you don't want to overcrowd the pan.

Plate up the sea bass fillets with the mango salsa spooned over the center. Serve immediately with a wedge of lime.

MONKFISH TAGINE WITH
PRESERVED LEMON & MINT

Fresh fish tagines are simply wonderful, redolent with spices and buttery sauces, often piquant with lemon and chiles/chillies and tempered with fresh herbs. The distinct Moroccan marinade chermoula is often used in fish dishes as the flavors of chile/chilli, cumin, and cilantro/coriander marry so well and complement the fish perfectly. Serve this tagine with chunks of fresh bread, or sautéed potatoes and a leafy salad.

2–3 tablespoons olive oil
1 red onion, finely chopped
2 carrots, finely chopped
2 celery stalks, finely chopped
1 preserved lemon, finely chopped
14-oz./400-g can of plum tomatoes
    with their juice
1¼ cups/300 ml fish stock or water
2 lb. 4 oz./1 kg fresh monkfish tail,
    cut into large chunks
a bunch of fresh mint leaves, finely
    shredded
sea salt and freshly ground black
    pepper
bread or sautéed potatoes, to serve

CHERMOULA
2–3 garlic cloves, chopped
1 red chile/chilli, deseeded and
    chopped
1 teaspoon sea salt
a small bunch of fresh cilantro/
    coriander
a pinch of saffron threads
1–2 teaspoons ground cumin
3–4 tablespoons olive oil
freshly squeezed juice of 1 lemon

SERVES 4–6

First make the chermoula. Using a mortar and pestle pound the garlic and chile/chilli with the salt to form a paste. Add the cilantro/coriander leaves and pound to a coarse paste. Beat in the saffron threads and cumin and bind well with the olive oil and lemon juice. Reserve 2 teaspoons of the chermoula for cooking. Toss the monkfish in the remaining chermoula, cover, and leave to marinate in the fridge for 1–2 hours.

Heat the oil in the base of a tagine or a heavy-based casserole. Stir in the onion, carrots, and celery and sauté for 2–3 minutes, until softened. Stir in half the preserved lemon, the reserved 2 teaspoons of chermoula, and the tomatoes.

Cook gently for about 10 minutes to reduce the liquid, then add the stock or water. Bring the liquid to the boil, cover the tagine, reduce the heat, and simmer for 10–15 minutes. Add the monkfish to the tagine, cover with the lid, and cook gently for 6–8 minutes, until the fish is cooked through.

Season with salt and pepper, sprinkle with the remaining preserved lemon and the shredded mint, and serve with chunks of fresh bread or sautéed potatoes and a leafy salad.

GOAN FISH CURRY

This curry starts with a masala spice blend. The key here is the blend of hot spice, sweet coconut, and a little sourness to balance the wonderful aromatic and satisfying flavors without overpowering the fish.

2 teaspoons brown sugar
2 teaspoons hot red pepper/chilli flakes
3 garlic cloves
1 tablespoon grated fresh ginger
1 brown onion, finely chopped
vegetable oil, for frying
scant ½ cup/140 g tomato paste/purée
1⅔ cups/400 ml canned coconut milk
1½ tablespoons/25 ml white wine vinegar
salt
6 red chiles/chillies, thinly sliced
14 oz./400 g firm white fish (such as plaice or pollock), chopped into bite-sized pieces
8 large uncooked shrimp/prawns, shells on
½ teaspoon mustard seeds
a small handful of dried curry leaves
boiled rice, to serve

MASALA SPICE BLEND
1 teaspoon whole cloves
1 tablespoon coriander seeds
1 teaspoon cumin seeds
3 black peppercorns
½ teaspoon ground turmeric
½ star anise

SERVES 4

Begin by making the masala spice blend. Preheat a skillet/frying pan over a medium heat. Put all of the spices in the dry pan and gently stir until they are strongly aromatic and starting to brown. Take off the heat and, using a mortar and pestle, grind the spices to a fine powder.

Add the sugar, hot red pepper/chilli flakes, garlic, ginger, and onion to the ground spices and mash together in the mortar and pestle.

Pour a little oil in a deep saucepan set over a medium heat. Add the spice mixture with the tomato paste/purée and cook until hot and bubbling. Slowly add the coconut milk and simmer for a couple of minutes—the mixture should be quite wet, like light/single cream; add a little water to thin it out if needed. Stir in the vinegar, taste, and season with a little salt.

Add the sliced fresh chile/chilli, then the fish pieces and shrimp/prawns. Cook until the shrimp/prawns are cooked through and pink in color.

In the pan you used to warm the spices, quickly fry the mustard seeds and curry leaves with a little vegetable oil until the mustard seeds start to pop in the heat. Scatter over the curry and serve with boiled rice.

OYSTER ROCKEFELLER HASH

Oyster Rockefeller—a dish of oysters, butter, breadcrumbs, and herbs—dates back to 1899 and was named after the richest man in the world at the time, John D. Rockefeller. Add it to potatoes for a hearty yet decadent dish.

6 tablespoons extra virgin olive oil
2 slices of white sandwich bread, processed into breadcrumbs
¾ teaspoon anise seeds
2 lb./1 kg Yukon Gold/Maris Piper potatoes, peeled and cut into ½-inch/1-cm cubes
1 onion, chopped
1 fennel bulb, cored and chopped
4 garlic cloves
1–2 pinches of cayenne pepper
10 oz./285 g frozen chopped spinach, thawed and squeezed dry
6 oz./170 g oysters, washed, drained, and coarsely chopped
4 eggs, at room temperature
salt and freshly ground black pepper

10-inch/25-cm cast-iron or non-stick skillet/frying pan

SERVES 4

Heat 2 tablespoons of the oil in the cast-iron or non-stick skillet/frying pan over a medium heat. Add the breadcrumbs to the hot oil. Sauté, stirring occasionally, until the crumbs are golden and crispy. Transfer to a bowl. Crush the anise seeds in the mortar and pestle, then mix with ½ teaspoon salt and ¼ teaspoon black pepper. Mix with the breadcrumbs and set aside.

Toss the potatoes with the oil in the pan, ½ teaspoon salt, and ¼ teaspoon pepper. Pan-fry the potatoes for about 5–7 minutes, until soft. Remove to a plate.

Add 4 tablespoons olive oil to the skillet/frying pan over a medium heat. Add the onion and fennel and sauté for 7-8 minutes, stirring occasionally, until softened. Crush the garlic in the mortar and pestle. Add to the pan with the cayenne pepper, 1 teaspoon salt, and ¼ teaspoon black pepper. Add the spinach, breaking it up. Add the potatoes, stir to combine, then press into a single layer. Cook for about 3 minutes (until the potatoes start to brown), then stir, press into a single layer again, and cook for another 3 minutes.

Add half the chopped oysters to the hash, stir and taste for seasoning. Reduce the heat to medium-low. Press the hash into a single layer a final time. Sprinkle the remaining oysters evenly over the surface of the hash. Using the back of a large spoon, make 4 indents in the hash. Crack an egg into each indent and season with salt and pepper. Cover the skillet/frying pan and cook until the eggs are just set, about 5 minutes.

Divide the hash into shallow bowls, taking care not to break the yolks. Sprinkle with the toasted breadcrumbs.

GRILLED LOBSTERS WITH
FLAVORED BUTTERS

Lobsters are so easy to throw on the grill or barbecue and serve up with an array of flavored butters. Steam the lobsters first and then put them on the grill, as this makes the meat juicy and tender.

4 cooked lobsters, about 2 lb./900 g each, steamed or boiled
oil, for brushing the grate
olive oil
sea salt and freshly ground black pepper
good crusty bread, to serve

NORI SEAWEED BUTTER
2 sheets of nori seaweed,
2 sticks/225 g salted butter

WASABI BUTTER
2 tablespoons wasabi powder
2 sticks/225 g salted butter

GARLIC & CHILE BUTTER
6 garlic cloves, peeled
1 jalapeño chile/chilli, roughly chopped
2 sticks/225 g salted butter

SERVES 4

To make the seaweed butter, crush the nori using a mortar and pestle, then add the butter and mix until smooth. Season with salt and pepper and spoon into a small bowl.

Mix together the wasabi and butter, then season with salt and pepper and spoon into a small bowl.

Lastly, crush the garlic and jalapeño using a mortar and pestle. Add the butter and mix to combine, season with salt and pepper, and spoon into a small bowl.

Heat the grill/barbecue to medium-high. Brush the grate with oil.

Crack the claws and brush the lobsters with olive oil, then season with salt and pepper. Using sharp scissors, cut the underneath of the lobster from top to bottom. Place the lobsters on the grill and cook for 5 minutes, then use tongs to turn them over and continue to cook for another 5 minutes or until the flesh is white and has no translucency.

Serve the lobsters with the flavored butters and plenty of crusty bread.

GARLIC CHILI SHRIMP

This is such an easy yet showstopping dish to serve for a casual supper—just set the large cast-iron pan in the middle of the table and eat the juicy shrimp/prawns with your hands, mopping up the juices with crusty rustic bread. You can use any type of shrimp/prawn that has the head and shell intact; simply increase the cooking time slightly for larger ones.

2 lb./900 g shrimp/prawns, heads on
1 whole head of garlic
1 tablespoon hot red pepper/
    chilli flakes
¼ cup/60 ml olive oil
2 tablespoons fresh oregano leaves
sea salt and cracked black pepper
good crusty bread, to serve

SERVES 4–6

Place the shrimp/prawns in a large bowl and set aside.

Break the garlic head into cloves, peel, and place in the mortar along with the hot red pepper/chilli flakes and olive oil. Crush with the pestle until the garlic is broken into small chunks.

Pour the garlic mixture over the shrimp/prawns and sprinkle with the oregano leaves. Season with salt and pepper and toss to combine. Set aside for 5 minutes.

Heat the grill/barbecue to medium–high.

Place a large cast-iron pan on the grill and heat until just smoking.

Place the shrimp/prawns and all the juices in the hot pan and cook for 6–8 minutes, turning every few minutes until they are cooked through. Cook a little longer if the shrimp/prawns are larger. Serve alongside a basket of crusty bread.

KAFFIR LIME, SQUID & NOODLE SALAD

This dish can be found in many guises, originating from Thailand, Vietnam, and Laos, as well as Cambodia. The squid is tenderized with a little salt, sugar, and lime juice and then grilled on skewers over hot coals or in a grill pan.

5 oz./150 g dried cellophane noodles

1 lb./500 g cleaned squid

½ teaspoon salt

½ teaspoon granulated/caster sugar

1 tablespoon freshly squeezed lime juice

2 snake beans (or a handful of green beans), trimmed and very thinly sliced

1 long red chile/chilli, deseeded and thinly sliced

2 red Asian shallots, thinly sliced

2 kaffir lime leaves, very thinly sliced

1 lemon grass stalk, trimmed and very thinly sliced

a small handful each of fresh mint, cilantro/coriander, and Thai basil leaves

deep-fried shallots, to serve

DRESSING

a handful of cilantro/coriander (stalks, leaves, and roots)

1 tablespoon freshly squeezed lime juice

2–3 teaspoons fish sauce

1–2 teaspoons granulated/caster sugar

6–8 bamboo skewers, soaked in cold water for 30 minutes

SERVES 4

Soak the noodles in a bowlful of hot water for 30 minutes until softened. Drain well, shake dry, and set aside in a large mixing bowl.

To make the dressing, pound the cilantro/coriander stalks, leaves, and roots together in a mortar and pestle (you need approximately a teaspoon of paste), then combine with all the other dressing ingredients in a small bowl. Stir well to dissolve the sugar.

Next prepare the squid. Cut the cleaned squid bodies in half and score the inside of the flesh with a sharp knife to make a diamond pattern. Cut into 2-inch/ 5-cm pieces. Put the squid in a large mixing bowl and add the salt, sugar, and lime juice, and rub well into the flesh. Set aside for 10 minutes, then thread the squid onto the pre-soaked skewers and set aside.

Meanwhile, put the remaining salad ingredients in a separate large mixing bowl, add 1 tablespoon of the dressing, and toss well to coat. Add the noodles and toss again to mix.

Preheat a stovetop ridged grill pan (or a heavy-based skillet/frying pan) over a high heat and when it starts to smoke, add the squid and cook for 1 minute on each side until charred. Remove the squid from the skewers and add to the noodles, drizzling the remaining dressing over the top. Toss well to coat and serve immediately, garnished with deep-fried shallots.

VEGETABLE DISHES & SALADS

MISO BORSCHT WITH
CITRUS & JUNIPER GREMOLATA

Traditionally, borscht is made with beet(root) and beef, but in this dense and filling soup the satisfying brothiness of miso replaces the meat.

1 cup/30 g dried porcini mushrooms
1 large onion
2 lb. 3 oz./1 kg beet(root), peeled
2 carrots
1 leek
500 g/1 lb. 2 oz. potatoes
2 tablespoons olive oil
4½ cups/300 g chestnut mushrooms, sliced
3 garlic cloves, finely chopped
½ small white cabbage, cored and shredded
1 tablespoon brown miso paste
3 tablespoons tomato paste/purée
a bunch of fresh dill, finely chopped
a bunch of fresh flat-leaf parsley, finely chopped
1 tablespoon runny honey
½ teaspoon hot red pepper/chilli flakes
½ cup/125 ml cider vinegar
sea salt and freshly ground black pepper
sour cream, to serve

CITRUS & JUNIPER GREMOLATA
5 juniper berries
zest of 1 lemon
zest of 1 orange
a handful of fresh flat-leaf parsley, finely chopped

SERVES 6–8

Place the dried mushrooms in a bowl and cover in boiling water to rehydrate for around 20 minutes. When they are plump and the liquid is dark, remove them and reserve the liquid.

Cut the onion, beet(root), carrots, leeks, and potatoes into ½-inch/1-cm chunks.

Heat the oil in a large heavy-based saucepan over a medium heat. Add the fresh mushrooms and onion and sauté until they begin to soften. Add the beet(root), carrots, leek, garlic, and 2 quarts/litres water. Strain in the mushroom soaking liquid to avoid adding the gritty residue at the bottom of the bowl.

Bring to the boil, then lower the heat and simmer for 5 minutes. Stir in the cabbage, potatoes, and rehydrated mushrooms. Add the miso paste and tomato paste/purée and return to the boil. Lower the heat and simmer until all the vegetables are cooked but with an al dente bite.

Remove the borscht from the heat. Stir in the dill, parsley (save a little to garnish), honey, hot red pepper/chilli flakes, and vinegar, and season with salt and pepper to taste (this may not be necessary).

To make the gremolata, grind the juniper berries in a mortar and pestle, then mix with the other ingredients in a bowl.

Serve the borscht with a dollop of sour cream, fresh parsley, and a sprinkle of gremolata.

BEAN TAGINE WITH HARISSA

This is a classic Berber tagine, which can be found in infinite variations throughout Morocco using different beans—haricot, borlotti, black-eyed, fava/broad, or butter beans. Often this dish is served on its own with chunks of bread, but it is also delicious served with thick, creamy yogurt and a Moroccan fruit chutney.

1 lb./450 g dried haricot beans, soaked in water overnight
4 garlic cloves, finely chopped
2 red chiles/chillies, deseeded and finely chopped
2–3 tablespoons ghee or argan oil, or 1 tablespoon olive oil plus 1 tablespoon butter
2 onions, finely chopped
2 teaspoons sugar
2 teaspoons harissa (see page 50)
2 x 14-oz./400-g cans of chopped tomatoes
a bunch of fresh mint leaves, finely chopped
a bunch of fresh flat-leaf parsley, finely chopped
a bunch of fresh cilantro/coriander, finely chopped
sea salt and freshly ground black pepper
1–2 lemons, cut into wedges, to serve

SERVES 4–6

Drain the soaked beans and place in a saucepan with plenty of fresh water and bring to the boil. Reduce the heat and simmer for about 30 minutes until the beans are tender. Drain thoroughly.

Crush the garlic and chiles/chillies using a mortar and pestle. Heat the ghee in the base of a tagine or in a heavy-based saucepan, add the onions, sugar and the garlic mixture and sauté for 2–3 minutes, until the onions begin to color. Stir in the harissa and toss in the drained beans. Add the tomatoes and top up with a little water to make sure the beans are submerged. Bring the liquid to the boil, reduce the heat, put on the lid, and cook gently for about 30 minutes.

Season the tagine with salt and pepper to taste, then stir in most of the herbs and simmer for a further 10 minutes.

Garnish with the remaining herbs and serve hot with the wedges of lemon to squeeze over the tagine.

BUTTERNUT SQUASH TAGINE

Variations of this sweet and spicy tagine are served in restaurants throughout Morocco, where the influences of the French, the Moors, and the Arabs are often evident in the cuisine. Enjoy the flavors of this tagine with a lemon or herb couscous and a tangy salad.

4 garlic cloves, peeled
2 tablespoons olive or argan oil
2 teaspoons fennel seeds
8–12 shallots, peeled and left whole
2–3 tablespoons golden raisins/
    sultanas
1–2 teaspoons harissa (see page 50)
1 butternut squash, peeled, deseeded
    and cut into bite-sized chunks
2 tablespoons honey
2 tablespoons pomegranate syrup
a small bunch of fresh cilantro/
    coriander, finely chopped
sea salt and freshly ground black
    pepper
1–2 tablespoons pomegranate seeds,
    to garnish

SERVES 4

Place the garlic in a mortar and crush with a pestle.

Heat the oil in the base of a tagine or in a heavy-based saucepan, stir in the crushed garlic and fennel seeds, and sauté for 1–2 minutes, until fragrant. Add the shallots, rolling them around in the oil, and cook for a further 2 minutes. Toss in the golden raisins/sultanas and cook until they plump up, then stir in the harissa and the butternut squash.

Pour in enough water to just cover the base of the tagine and bring it to the boil. Put on the lid and cook the tagine over a medium heat for 15 minutes, until the butternut squash is tender. Stir in the honey and pomegranate syrup and cook over a medium heat for a further 10 minutes.

Season the tagine with salt and pepper, stir in most of the cilantro/coriander, then garnish with the remaining herbs and the pomegranate seeds.

FRESH LIME, VEGETABLE & COCONUT CURRY

This Thai coconut curry uses a delicious and easily made paste as its base. The vegetables don't need to be cooked for too long, otherwise they will lose their lovely vibrant color and crispy texture.

2 x 14-fl. oz./400-ml cans of full-fat coconut milk
scant ½ cup/100 ml well-flavored vegetable stock
1 tablespoon turbinado/demerara sugar
3½ oz./100 g cherry tomatoes, roughly chopped
1 yellow (bell) pepper, deseeded and cut into strips
14 oz./400 g mixed young vegetables (sugar snap peas, green beans, long-stem broccoli, baby corn/ sweetcorn, etc.)
a small bunch of fresh cilantro/ coriander, roughly chopped
zest and juice of 1 large lime
a handful of cashew nuts, to serve
a bunch of scallions/spring onions, thinly sliced, to serve

CURRY PASTE
1½ oz./45 g piece of fresh ginger
2 garlic cloves
1 stalk of lemon grass, trimmed
3 kaffir lime leaves
1 tablespoon ground coriander
1 tablespoon ground cumin
1 scant tablespoon hot red pepper/ chilli flakes
1 tablespoon coconut oil
a bunch of fresh cilantro/coriander

SERVES 4

To make the curry paste, peel the ginger and garlic, then roughly chop along with the lemon grass. Place in a mortar and bash them into a paste using the pestle. Add the lime leaves, ground coriander, cumin, hot red pepper/chilli flakes, and coconut oil. Pour in 1-2 tablespoons of warm water and mix everything to a paste. Roughly chop the cilantro/coriander, add to the mortar, and pound until everything is ground down and evenly mixed.

Preheat the oven to 350°F (180°C) Gas 4.

For the curry, pour the coconut milk and stock into a deep roasting pan and stir in the curry paste and sugar. Cover with kitchen foil and cook for 15 minutes.

Remove the roasting pan from the oven, give it a good stir, and add the chopped tomatoes, (bell) pepper strips, and prepared vegetables (cut the baby corn/ sweetcorn in half from top to bottom, if using). Replace the foil over the pan, return it to the oven, and cook for 10 minutes or so, until the vegetables are just soft but retain their bright colors.

Stir in the fresh cilantro/coriander and add the lime zest and juice. Serve straight away, scattered with cashews and scallions/spring onions.

PANEER KADHAI

This recipe is a north Indian, Punjabi-style dish that is an absolute winner for vegetarians. Paneer is an Indian set cheese similar to cottage cheese in texture but also quite like halloumi in regards to its firmness. Before adding it to the sauce, shallow-fry the cheese cubes on all sides because the caramelized edges add a lovely "nutty" flavor. Translated, "kadhai" means "wok," which is the best pan to use—you want the oil to be smoking hot to create a flavorsome curry.

4 tablespoons vegetable oil
1 lb. 2 oz./500 g paneer, diced
1 teaspoon coriander seeds
1 teaspoon ginger paste
1-inch/2.5-cm piece of fresh ginger,
    cut into matchsticks
1 large onion, cut into 8 wedges
2 teaspoons salt
½ teaspoon ground turmeric
2 large tomatoes, finely chopped
    (core and seeds removed)
2 teaspoons tomato paste/purée
1 whole red (bell) pepper, deseeded
    and cut into wedges
1 whole green (bell) pepper,
    deseeded and cut into wedges
1 teaspoon dried fenugreek leaves
2 tablespoons freshly chopped
    cilantro/coriander (leaves from
    a small bunch)
2–3 fresh green chiles/chillies,
    sliced

KADHAI SPICE
1 teaspoon whole coriander seeds
3 dried chiles/chillies

SERVES 5

For the kadhai spice, toast the coriander seeds and chiles/chillies in a pan over a medium heat until the spices become fragrant and aromatic. Pound using a mortar and pestle. (You will need 2 teaspoons of the spice blend.)

In a large wok over a medium heat, heat the vegetable oil and seal the paneer on all sides. Remove from the pan, drain on paper towels, and set aside.

Keeping the oil in the pan, fry the coriander seeds until they begin to sizzle. Add the ginger paste and fresh ginger and stir-fry until they start to brown slightly. Add the onion wedges and salt and stir-fry until they are cooked through but not too soft (this is a stir-fry dish, so you want the vegetables to retain a little bite).

Add 2 teaspoons of the kadhai spice blend and the turmeric and mix well for 1 minute. Add the tomatoes and tomato paste/purée and cook through until the tomatoes have melted and softened.

Add the (bell) peppers and ¾ cup/200 ml water, mix well, and cook through over a low heat with the lid on for 3–4 minutes. The sauce needs to coat the vegetables, so it shouldn't be too runny. Add the paneer and fenugreek leaves and mix well.

Garnish the kadhai with freshly chopped cilantro/coriander and green chiles/chillies and serve.

HONEY & RAS EL HANOUT ROOTS WITH PISTACHIOS

Pungent ras el hanout spice mix, vibrant green pistachios, and juicy pomegranate seeds add a punch of flavor to roasted root vegetables.

10½ oz./300 g celery root/celeriac
10½ oz./300 g parsnips
10½ oz./300 g carrots
5½ oz./150 g baby turnips
7 oz./200 g beets/beetroots
7 oz./200 g butternut squash
7 oz./200 g shallots, peeled
3¾ tablespoons/50 ml olive oil
2 tablespoons ras el hanout
1 tablespoon runny honey
1¾ oz./50 g pistachios
seeds from 1 pomegranate
sea salt and freshly ground black
    pepper
fresh parsley, to garnish

RAS EL HANOUT SPICE MIX
⅓ oz./10 g coarsely ground black
    pepper
⅓ oz./10 g ground coriander
1 tablespoon/5 g ground ginger
1 tablespoon/5 g smoked paprika
½ teaspoon each allspice, ground
    nutmeg, ground turmeric, and
    cayenne pepper
seeds from 2 green cardamom pods
¼ teaspoon ground cloves
1 teaspoon dried rose petals

YOGURT DRESSING
6¾ fl. oz./200 ml sheep's milk yogurt
1 garlic clove, peeled and grated
a handful of freshly chopped
    cilantro/coriander

SERVES 4

Preheat the oven to 350°F (180°C) Gas 4.

To make the ras el hanout spice mix, grind all the spices together using a mortar and pestle. Store in a screw-top jar.

Peel and dice the celery root/celeriac. Cut the parsnips and carrots into batons. Cut the baby turnips, beets/beetroots, and butternut squash into wedges. Toss them together in a large sheet pan. Add the shallots. Mix the olive oil with the ras el hanout spice mix (store the remainder in a screw-top jar), and stir in the honey. Pour this over the vegetables, season with salt and freshly ground black pepper, and toss to coat everything evenly.

Roast in the preheated oven for about 30–35 minutes, until the vegetables are soft and charred a little here and there. Remove from the oven, transfer to a warm serving dish, and scatter over the pistachios and pomegranate seeds.

For the dressing, mix the sheep's milk yogurt with the grated garlic and chopped cilantro/coriander, and spoon a little of the mix here and there. Garnish with fresh parsley and serve warm.

BERBERE CAULIFLOWER WITH
APRICOTS, PINE NUTS & MUHAMMARA

Berbere is a punchy hot spice mix from Ethiopia and muhammara is a glorious,
dip-into or dollop-on invention that hails from Aleppo in Syria.

a good-sized cauliflower
3–4 tablespoons olive oil
1½ tablespoons berbere spice mix
scant ½ cup/50 g toasted pine nuts
1⅓ cups/200 g dried apricots, halved

MUHAMMARA
2 red (bell) peppers, deseeded
3 tablespoons olive oil
1 teaspoon ground cumin
½ cup/50 g walnut pieces
1 garlic clove, finely chopped
½ cup/30 g fresh breadcrumbs
1 tablespoon pomegranate molasses
1 tablespoon tomato ketchup
1 teaspoon red pepper/chilli flakes
sea salt and ground black pepper

BERBERE SPICE MIX
1 oz./30 g red pepper/chilli flakes
¼ oz./8 g each flaked sea salt,
    coarsely ground black pepper,
    ground cumin, and coriander seeds
a large pinch of fenugreek powder
a small pinch of ground ginger
⅓ teaspoon each allspice, ground
    cloves, and ground nutmeg
seeds from 2 green cardamom pods

TO SERVE
2 tablespoons pomegranate molasses
3 tablespoons olive oil
a handful of cilantro/coriander,
    parsley, and mint, chopped

SERVES 4

Preheat the oven to 375°F (190°C) Gas 5.

To make the muhammara, cut the red (bell) peppers
into strips. Toss with 2 tablespoons of the oil and the
cumin and arrange the strips over a large sheet pan.
Roast in the preheated oven for about 20 minutes,
until softened and slightly charred. Transfer to a
blender and whiz to a purée. Add the walnuts, garlic,
breadcrumbs, pomegranate molasses, ketchup, red
pepper/chilli flakes, and remaining oil and whiz again,
until you have a lightly textured purée with the
consistency of whipped cream. If the mixture is a little
too thick, add some warm water. Season and set aside.

For the berbere spice mix, grind the spices together
using a mortar and pestle, until you have a lightly
textured powder. (Unused spice mix can be stored in
a screw-top jar.)

Break the cauliflower into small florets and toss in
a bowl with the olive oil and berbere spice mix.

Spread over the sheet pan used for the (bell) peppers
and roast for about 15 minutes, until the cauliflower is
cooked, but still has a little bite. Scatter over the pine
nuts and apricots and return to the oven for a few
minutes to warm through.

Stir the pomegranate molasses and oil together and
spoon over the cauliflower. Scatter with the freshly
chopped herbs and serve with the muhammara.

CHARRED HISPI CABBAGE
WITH CHERRY & JUNIPER BUTTER

When cabbage comes out of the oven, still with a little bite, its sweet flavor intensified against crisp, charred edges, you should prepare yourself for a treat.

1 hispi/pointed cabbage, trimmed
3–4 tablespoons olive oil
9-oz./250 g pouch of pre-cooked freekeh
zest and freshly squeezed juice of 1 lemon
sea salt and freshly ground black pepper
freshly chopped parsley, to garnish

CHERRY & JUNIPER BUTTER
20 juniper berries
½ cup minus 1 tablespoon/100 g salted butter, softened
1 generous teaspoon freshly chopped rosemary
1¾ oz./50 g dried cherries, roughly chopped

SERVES 3–4

Crush the juniper berries using a mortar and pestle. Add the butter, rosemary, and dried cherries to the juniper berries, and work together until everything is evenly mixed.

Lay a piece of plastic wrap/clingfilm on a clean work surface. Form the butter into a small sausage shape, and roll up in the plastic wrap/clingfilm. Give the package a little roll backwards and forwards to create an even shape and swizzle the ends to seal. Transfer to the fridge to firm up.

Preheat the oven to 375°F (190°C) Gas 5.

Cut the cabbage in half from root to tip, and then cut each half into three or four wedges. Arrange them on a sheet pan and drizzle with half of the oil. Bake in the preheated oven for 10 minutes. Remove the pan from the oven, scatter over the freekeh, and drizzle over the remaining olive oil.

Return to the oven and cook for a further 5 minutes or so, until the freekeh is hot and crisp and the edges of the cabbage are lightly charred. Remove from the oven, scatter over the lemon zest and juice, season with salt and black pepper, and garnish with freshly chopped parsley. Serve while hot, with thin slices of the cherry and juniper butter melting into the leaves.

ROASTED BEETS & CARROTS
WITH WALNUT SKORDALIA

This is a dish that is a great mezze, appetizer, or side. Or make it a main meal by serving with crumbled feta and a handful of arugula/rocket.

2–3 beets/beetroots (approx. 1 lb. 2 oz./500 g), scrubbed and cut into wedges
5 mixed purple and orange carrots (approx. 1 lb. 2 oz./500 g), scrubbed and cut into 3 pieces
2 tablespoons olive oil
6 sprigs of oregano or 1 teaspoon dried oregano
sea salt and freshly ground black pepper

SKORDALIA
1 potato, peeled and cut into cubes
3 garlic cloves, peeled
¾ cup/100 g walnuts, lightly toasted (some reserved to garnish)
½ tablespoon red wine vinegar
2 tablespoons olive oil
sea salt and freshly ground black pepper

SERVES 4–6 AS A SIDE

To make the skordalia, place the potato in a small saucepan of water, bring to the boil, and cook until very soft. Drain, reserving some of the cooking water.

Using a mortar and pestle, crush the garlic with the walnuts until they are fully combined and become a creamy consistency. Add the garlic and walnut mixture and the vinegar to the potatoes. When they are thoroughly combined, add the oil and mix by hand until you achieve the desired taste. Season with salt and pepper. Place in the fridge for at least 1 hour before you serve. You might find you need a little more vinegar or olive oil to get an appetizing texture and balance of flavors.

Preheat the oven to 350°F (180°C) Gas 4.

Place the beets/beetroot and carrots on a baking sheet. Drizzle over the olive oil and sprinkle with oregano, salt, and pepper. Bake in the preheated oven for 50–65 minutes until cooked through and crispy around the edges. Remove from the oven and serve the vegetables heaped on a bed of skordalia, finished with a scattering of the reserved walnuts.

ZUCCHINI & MUSHROOMS A LA GRECQUE

This dish offers a modern twist on the classic French way of serving a vegetable salad with a hot wine-based dressing. Pour the dressing over the vegetables rather than cook them in it, as this makes for brighter colors and a fresher, crunchier texture. If you wish, tone down the heat by using fewer chiles/chillies.

1¼ cups/300 ml crisp, dry white wine
2 garlic cloves, very finely chopped
2 bay leaves
1 tablespoon coriander seeds
1 teaspoon coarse sea salt, plus extra for seasoning
½ teaspoon black peppercorns
¼–½ teaspoon crushed dried chiles/chillies, to taste
5 tablespoons/75 ml extra virgin olive oil
1–2 tablespoons freshly squeezed lemon juice
9 oz./250 g small zucchini/courgettes
12 oz./350 g button mushrooms
2 rounded tablespoons freshly chopped mint leaves
2 rounded tablespoons freshly chopped parsley
freshly ground black pepper
warm pitta bread or other flatbread, to serve

SERVES 4

Heat the wine, garlic, and bay leaves in a small saucepan and simmer gently until the wine has reduced by half. Remove and discard the bay leaves.

Grind the coriander seeds, sea salt, peppercorns, and dried chiles/chillies using a mortar and pestle. Add this to the reduced wine, along with the olive oil and 1 tablespoon of lemon juice. Stir and simmer over a very low heat for 4–5 minutes.

Meanwhile, top and tail the zucchini/courgettes and cut them lengthways into very thin slices using a mandolin or a vegetable peeler. Wipe the mushrooms and slice them thickly. Put the vegetables in a large, heatproof serving bowl, pour over the hot dressing and sprinkle with the mint leaves. Toss the vegetables in the dressing, then let cool for about 1 hour, tossing them occasionally.

Check the seasoning, adding more salt, pepper, and lemon juice, if necessary. Add the parsley, toss well, and serve with warm pitta bread or other flatbread.

PURPLE SAUERKRAUT
WITH DULSE & CARAWAY SEEDS

This red cabbage fermented into a purple kraut will brighten up any meal! The seaweed contains vital minerals, while caraway seeds make it very aromatic. Try this combination—you won't be disappointed!

1½ teaspoons caraway seeds
½ oz./10 g dulse seaweed
1 medium head red cabbage (approx. 28 oz./800 g in weight), very finely chopped or shredded/grated
2½ teaspoons salt

sterilized glass jar, pickle press, or crock (see page 4)

MAKES 2 CUPS/200 G

Use a mortar and pestle to crush the caraway seeds.

Place the dulse in a bowl, cover with water, and let it soak for 10 minutes, then drain and chop.

Place the cabbage and salt in a large bowl and squeeze with clean hands—this will help to release the juices. Add the seaweed and crushed caraway seeds.

The cabbage should be dripping wet. To ensure proper fermentation without the presence of oxygen, carefully pack the spiced cabbage with its juice in a big jar, pickle press, or crock. It should always be submerged in its own brine, so stuff it tightly and screw down the lid of the pickle press as much as you can, or if using a jar or crock, pack tightly, cover with a plate that fits inside, and place a weight on top.

Check after 12 hours and press again; the cabbage will wilt further and more juice will come out. The shortest fermentation time for the process to start is 3 days, but it is best left for at least 7 days and ideally for 4 weeks. During fermentation, check every other day and remove any foam and/or mold that might form on the surface of the brine—a common occurrence that will not in any way affect the quality of your sauerkraut.

After 4 weeks transfer the sauerkraut to sterilized jars, cover in brine, and refrigerate. It will stay fresh for at least 1 month and possibly 2–3 months. Bring to room temperature before eating.

CHICKPEA, SQUASH & SPINACH SALAD WITH DUKKAH

Dukkah is a fragrant Egyptian mix of spices, nuts, and seeds, delicious sprinkled over salads or roasted vegetables, or stirred into olive oil for a quick and easy dip to serve with flatbreads.

1 teaspoon smoked hot paprika
1 tablespoon extra virgin olive oil
14 oz./400 g butternut squash, peeled, seeded and sliced into wedges
5 oz./150 g baby spinach leaves, tough stalks trimmed
2 avocados, peeled, halved, pitted/stoned, and cubed
14-oz./400-g can of chickpeas, drained and rinsed
1 small red onion, diced
a large handful of cilantro/coriander leaves
2 tablespoons dukkah (see page 134)
sea salt and freshly ground black pepper

LEMON-CORIANDER DRESSING
1 teaspoon coriander seeds
5 tablespoons extra virgin olive oil
finely grated zest and freshly squeezed juice of 1 small lemon

SERVES 4

Preheat the oven to 400°F (200°C) Gas 6.

Mix the paprika with the oil in a large bowl, season, stir in the squash, and turn until evenly coated. Roast the squash in the preheated oven for 30–35 minutes, turning once, until tender and golden.

For the dressing, put the coriander seeds in a large, dry skillet/frying pan and toast for 2–3 minutes, shaking the pan occasionally, until they smell aromatic and start to colour. Grind using a mortar and pestle to a coarse powder, then mix in the oil and lemon zest and juice. Season and set aside.

Put the spinach in a large serving bowl and add the roasted squash, avocados, chickpeas, red onion, and half the fresh cilantro/coriander. Pour enough of the dressing over to coat and turn gently until combined.

Just before serving, sprinkle 2 tablespoons of the dukkah and the remaining cilantro/coriander over.

SHAVED BROCCOLI & BUCKWHEAT SALAD

WITH DUKKAH TOPPING

This salad uses the often forgotten broccoli stems, shaved into strips. Buckwheat, a great supergrain, works well in this dish but wheatberries would be just as good. Dukkah is a special addition to any salad—make it in bulk and keep a big batch in the fridge.

1 cup/250 ml vegetable stock
1 cup/185 g buckwheat groats
4 broccoli stalks
⅛ cup/15 g chopped hazelnuts

DRESSING
1 cup/300 g plain yogurt
freshly squeezed juice of 2 lemons
½ teaspoon sea salt
½ teaspoon cumin powder
a bunch of fresh cilantro/coriander,
    chopped

DUKKAH
2 teaspoons cumin seeds
2 teaspoons coriander seeds
1 teaspoon fennel seeds
¾ cup/100 g roasted hazelnuts,
    chopped
¾ cup/100 g roasted sunflower seeds,
    chopped
1 teaspoon sea salt

SERVES 4–6

In a large saucepan or pot, put the vegetable stock, 1 cup/250 ml water and buckwheat groats over a medium-high heat. Bring to the boil, then turn down the heat and simmer for 15 minutes with the lid half on, stirring once halfway through. Be careful not to overcook the groats. Drain and rinse with cold water, then set aside in a bowl to cool.

Peel and shave the broccoli stalks into ribbons using a vegetable peeler or mandolin, then add to a large saucepan or pot of boiling water. Cook for 3 minutes, then drain and submerge the broccoli in a bowl of iced water to stop the cooking process. Drain, cool, and mix with the hazelnuts and reserved buckwheat.

For the dressing, whisk all the ingredients together and store in the fridge until you are ready to serve.

For the dukkah topping, use a mortar and pestle to grind the cumin, coriander, and fennel seeds. Stir in the hazelnuts and sunflower seeds, then mix in a bowl with the crushed spices and set aside. This should yield about 1½ cups/200 g of dukkah—any leftover can be stored in a screw-top jar.

To serve, spoon the broccoli and buckwheat mix onto individual plates, drizzle over the dressing, and cover each serving with a tablespoon of dukkah topping

CHARRED TREVISO SALAD

Charred Treviso bathed in an anchovy and almond dressing is a delicious accompaniment to any cookout. It's a hardy but milder relative of radicchio and has pretty, long leaves tinged with green and white. The anchovies and breadcrumbs add sweetness to this salad.

½ cup/55 g almonds, roughly chopped
2-oz/56-g can of anchovies
2 cups/100 g panko breadcrumbs
3 tablespoons salted capers
¼ cup/60 ml olive oil
4 small Treviso chicory/radicchio, cut in half lengthwise
¼ cup/30 g grated Parmesan cheese (optional)
cracked black pepper
oil, for brushing the grate

SERVES 6–8

Place the almonds and anchovies (there's no need to drain them) in a mortar and use the pestle to pound to a rough consistency. Pour the mixture into a bowl and add the breadcrumbs, capers, and half the olive oil. Toss together and season with black pepper.

Heat a pan over a medium-high heat, add the breadcrumb mixture, and toast until golden brown. Set aside.

Heat the grill/barbecue to medium-high. Brush the grate with oil. Place the Treviso on a baking sheet and brush with the remaining olive oil. Grill for 2–3 minutes on each side until slightly charred and wilted.

Remove them to a platter and scatter with the breadcrumb mix. Sprinkle with the Parmesan, if using, and season with a little more black pepper.

WATERMELON & RICOTTA SALATA SALAD WITH OLIVE SALT

This is a delightfully pretty, refreshing salad in which the olive salt brings out the sweetness of the watermelon. Ricotta salata, a lightly salted cheese made from sheep milk, originates from the island of Sicily. If you can't find a mini watermelon, buy the smallest available and cut it in half. You can use Greek feta cheese if ricotta salata isn't available (or see the recipe on page 141).

1 mini seedless watermelon
6 oz./170 g ricotta salata cheese
2 tablespoons fresh oregano leaves
olive oil, to drizzle
cracked black pepper, to season

OLIVE SALT
10 black olives, pitted/stoned
2½ tablespoons sea salt

SERVES 2

Peel the watermelon and cut it into bite-size chunks. Put in a serving bowl, crumble the ricotta salata over the watermelon, and sprinkle with the oregano.

To make the olive salt, chop the olives roughly. Grind them with the salt using a mortar and pestle until the olives are mashed.

Drizzle the olive oil over the salad and season with black pepper. Sprinkle with a generous amount of the olive salt. Put the remainder of the salt in a bowl to use on other dishes.

GRILLED TOMATO CAPRESE

Making your own ricotta is a breeze and absolutely delicious. The same goes for pesto—try this and you won't buy readymade again. This salad is perfect for a summer lunch, served with grilled breads and chilled rosé.

2 lb./900 g cherry tomatoes (about 6 branches)
basil leaves, for garnishing
oil, for brushing the grate

RICOTTA
8 cups/1.9 litres whole milk
1 cup/250 ml heavy/double cream
⅓ cup/80 ml organic white distilled vinegar or freshly squeezed lemon juice

PESTO
2 cups/100 g fresh basil leaves
½ cup/35 g freshly grated Parmesan cheese
½ cup/55 g chopped almonds
2 garlic cloves, minced
½ cup/125 ml extra virgin olive oil
1 tablespoon freshly squeezed lemon juice
salt and freshly ground black pepper

candy thermometer

large strainer/sieve

cheesecloth/muslin

SERVES 6–8

To make the ricotta, pour the milk and cream into a large pan and place over a medium heat. Place a candy thermometer on the side of the pan and heat to 190°F (88°C).

Remove the pan from the heat and add the vinegar or lemon juice. Using a wooden spoon, stir the mixture very slowly a few times, then cover with a dish towel and set aside for 1 hour.

Line a strainer/sieve with cheesecloth/muslin and place over a bowl large enough to catch the whey. Gently pour the ricotta curds into the cheesecloth and let drain for 45 minutes. Place the ricotta in a glass storage container and season with salt and pepper, then cover and refrigerate.

To make the pesto, place the basil, cheese, almonds, and garlic in the mortar and pound a couple of times with the pestle. Pour in the olive oil in a steady stream, continuing to pound. Add the lemon juice and season with salt and pepper. Pound a few times to combine, then pour into a glass storage container.

Heat the grill/barbecue to medium-high. Brush the grate with oil.

Place the tomatoes on the grill and cook for about 4 minutes until they are bursting open and charred.

To serve, spoon the ricotta onto a platter and top with the grilled tomatoes, then drizzle with the pesto and garnish with the basil. Store the remaining pesto in the fridge for another use—it will keep for up to a week.

INDEX

CREDITS

RECIPE CREDITS

VALERIE AIKMAN-SMITH
Charred treviso salad
Garlic chili shrimp
Grilled harissa chicken kabobs
Grilled lobsters with flavored
  butters
Grilled tomato caprese
Indian-spiced leg of lamb cooked
  in a salt crust
Lemon & dill mustard
Médoc mustard
Provençal olive relish
Rosemary & thyme mustard
Salt-cured gravadlax with caper
  sauce
Watermelon & ricotta salata salad
  with olive salt
Wholegrain mustard

LOUISE PICKFORD
Balachung myanmar
Chiang mai beef noodle curry
Chicken laksa
Green nam jim
Hot & sour fish soup
Kaffir lime, squid & noodle salad
Nuoc cham
Seared duck laos with cucumber
  noodle salad

MAT FOLLAS
Dill & lemon pesto
Goan fish curry
Kale pesto
Slow-roasted garlic, cheese &
  szechuan peppercorn toasts
Traditional pesto
Wild garlic pesto

GHILLIE BASAN
Baked lamb tagine with quinces,
  figs & honey
Bean tagine with harissa
Butternut squash tagine
Chicken tagine with harissa,
  artichokes & green grapes
Monkfish tagine with preserved
  lemon & mint

LIZ FRANKLIN
Berbere cauliflower with apricots,
  pine nuts & muhammara
Charred hispi cabbage with cherry
  & juniper butter
Fresh lime, vegetable & coconut
  curry
Honey & ras el hanout roots with
  pistachios
Polenta fries with pesto

JORDAN BOURKE
Pan-fried chickpea fritters
Pulled lamb shoulder with orange
  & cinnamon pilaff
Quail with borlotti beans, baby
  tomatoes & salmoriglio
Spice-crusted sea bass with mango
  salsa

CHLOE COKER & JANE MONTGOMERY
Mushroom & walnut pesto
Ricotta & herb pesto
Roasted beet pesto
Watercress pesto

CAROL HILKER
Baked parmesan wings
Oyster rockefeller hash
Spiced pulled pork hash
Yuzu pao chicken wings

JAMES PORTER
Beef tri-tip poke
Fish tacos
Furikake popcorn
Red salsa

FIONA BECKETT
Italian-style roast pork with white
  wine, garlic & fennel
Pepper-crusted steaks with red
  wine sauce
Zucchini & mushrooms à la grecque

PHILIP DENNHARDT & KRISTIN JENSEN
Gremolata
Pounded parsley & garlic oil
Salsa verde

NITISHA PATEL
Goan pork vindaloo
Paneer kadhai
Slow-roasted leg of lamb

LAURA SANTTINI
Miso borscht with citrus & juniper
  gremolata
Smoked mackerel with pink pepper
  & squid ink spaghetti
Umami steak tagliata

KATHY KORDALIS
Roasted beets & carrots with walnut
  skordalia
Stuffed porchetta

URSULA FERRIGNO
Pasta with sardines

AMY RUTH FINEGOLD
Shaved broccoli & buckwheat salad
  with dukkah topping

FELIPE FUENTES CRUZ & BEN FORDHAM
Roasted tomatillo salsa

NICOLA GRAIMES
Chickpea, squash & spinach salad
  with dukkah

DUNJA GULIN
Purple sauerkraut with dulse
  & carraway seeds

JENNY LINFORD
Malaysian chicken & potato curry

JANET SAWYER
Coconut & vanilla chicken curry

LAURA WASHBURN-HUTTON
Matchstick fries with sichuan
  pepper salt

PHOTOGRAPHY CREDITS

JAN BALDWIN
Pages 3, 109

MARTIN BRIGDALE
Pages 48, 68

PETER CASSIDY
Pages 5, 34, 37, 97

TARA FISHER
Pages 32, 54, 73, 94

JONATHAN GREGSON
Pages 1, 6, 71, 85

MOWIE KAY
Pages 15, 19, 27, 35, 59, 63, 75, 76,
  86, 88, 127, 128

ERIN KUNKEL
Pages 51, 77, 102, 105, 140

DAVID MUNNS
Pages 36, 56, 90

STEVE PAINTER
Pages 10, 28, 31, 43, 98, 112, 115, 116,
  120, 123, 124

CON POULOS
Pages 79, 111

WILLIAM REAVELL
Endpapers, pages 9, 12

MATT RUSSELL
Page 132

CHRISTOPHER SCHOLEY
Pages 24, 82, 83, 93, 108

TOBY SCOTT
Pages 44, 47, 64, 101, 131

IAN WALLACE
Back cover, pages 2, 20, 23, 39, 52,
  80, 89, 106

KATE WHITAKER
Spine, page 25

CLARE WINFIELD
Front cover, pages 8, 40, 57, 60, 67,
  72, 119, 135